"Chrissy Schofield is ⋯ h tragedy. She finds joy, beauty, ⋯ rrow. She is so close to God th ⋯ er kitchen table, having breakfa ⋯ y, you will feel good about life and closer to ⋯ rumptious writer; I drool over everything that comes from her tablet, and this story is a treasure."

> Daniel Schantz, professor of Christian education, Central Christian College of the Bible, Moberly, Missouri

"I've read many books and articles about lives interrupted in ways that forever shift the meaning of 'normal,' but never have I been so personally impacted by such an account. Christina Schofield shares an insider's view of such a shift with clarity, honesty and a God given wit that brings tears and laughter, awe and reverence. She doesn't sugarcoat her family's struggle, but deals candidly with doubt and uncertainty in a way that coaxes readers to face their own fears and your uncertainties. Her questions come from a heart sincerely searching for answers and yearning to know God's will.

"Christina's story caused me to reexamine my own heart, and to review all I know of God's amazing character—His faithfulness, mercy, kindness, compassion and so much more. Truly a life-changing book, a page-turner in the very best sense; a courageous story about a couple who did not choose this path yet have anchored themselves to God, anticipating that some way, somehow, He will turn their experience into something lovely. I believe He already has."

> Bonnie Bruno, author, *When God Steps In: Stories of Everyday Grace* and *The Young Reader's Bible*; www.bonniebruno.com

"I love this book and I encourage anyone to read it. Somehow Christina has found a way to write about her painful story with surprising honesty, humility and humor. But don't be fooled: This book is not about her. God is the main character, and cover to cover, this is a relatable story of His faithfulness to all of us in our suffering."

Amy Simpson, vice president, *Christianity Today*;
publisher and editor-in-chief, Kyria.com

"Some people like to wrap faith up in a box with perfect pretty paper and tie it in a bow, nice and neat. But real life isn't like that—when difficulties come, that false, prepackaged faith crumbles apart. Real life can be messy, painful and confusing—real life demands a real faith. That's the kind of faith you'll find in this book.

"Christina is as real as it gets: honest, gutsy, authentic, raw. And through it all—journeying day-by-day through tragedy and its aftermath—she's courageously joyful. Whether you're facing tragedy, a fearful situation or just the everyday jumble of difficulties, questions and emotional challenges that life throws our way, you can find hope and inspiration (and some hysterical laughs!) as you journey with Christina through the pages of this book. What a privilege it is to watch Christina and Allen as they walk together with Jesus."

Kelli B. Trujillo, author, *Faith-Filled Moments* and *The Busy Mom's Guide to Spiritual Survival*

MY
LIFE and
Lesser Catastrophes

MY
LIFE *and*
Lesser Catastrophes

NORTHFIELD PUBLIC LIBRARY
210 Washington Street
Northfield, MN 55057

Christina Schofield

Northfield Public Library
Northfield, Minnesota

Gift Presented by

a division of Baker Publishing Group
Minneapolis, Minnesota

*Hiram Scriver
Memorial Fund*

1\/\|

Copyright © 2011 by Christina Schofield

Published by Chosen Books
a division of Baker Publishing Group
11400 Hampshire Avenue South, Bloomington, MN 55438
www.chosenbooks.com

Cover design by Dan Pitts

Printed in the United States of America

All rights reserved. No part of this publication may be reproduced, stored in a retrieval system or transmitted in any form or by any means—electronic, mechanical, photocopying, recording or otherwise—without the prior written permission of the publisher. The only exception is brief quotations in printed reviews.

Library of Congress Cataloging-in-Publication Data
Schofield, Christina (Christina Diane).
    My life and lesser catastrophes : an unflinchingly honest journey of faith /
Christina Schofield.
        p. cm.
    ISBN 978-0-8007-9511-5 (pbk. : alk. paper)
    1. Schofield, Christina (Christina Diane), 1972– 2. Schofield, Allen. 3. Christian biography—United States. I. Title.
BR1725.S376A3 2011
277.3′083092—dc22   2011002961

Unless otherwise identified, Scripture quotations are from the HOLY BIBLE, NEW INTERNATIONAL VERSION.® Copyright © 1973, 1978, 1984 Biblica. Used by permission of Zondervan. All rights reserved.

Scripture quotations identified NLT are from the Holy Bible, New Living Translation, copyright © 1996, 2004. Used by permission of Tyndale House Publishers, Inc., Wheaton, Illinois 60189. All rights reserved.

Scripture quotations identified TNIV are from the HOLY BIBLE, TODAY'S NEW INTERNATIONAL VERSION.® TNIV.® Copyright © 2001, 2005 by Biblica. Used by permission of Biblica.® All rights reserved worldwide.

Scripture quotations identified KJV are from the King James Version of the Bible.

11   12   13   14   15   16   17   7   6   5   4   3   2   1

to Dad and Mom,

my beloved parents, and to brave, strong Allen.

CONTENTS

Acknowledgments 11

1. On the Skids 13
2. Groans and Grimaces 21
3. Stale Cracker Philosophy 29
4. Thick-and-Thin Hope 41
5. Give-and-Take 51
6. The Invisible Hand 61
7. Still Calming Storms 69
8. A Doting Dad 77
9. The Whispers of God 87
10. Fried Chicken and Priorities 95
11. Climbs and Plunges 103
12. Valuable Ruins 111
13. Getting Places 119
14. Desperate Measures 129
15. Mighty Seed 139
16. Rhino Revelations 147

ACKNOWLEDGMENTS

One morning, in the aftermath of our calamity, I slipped away to our church's dark, musty basement to be alone with God and to pray. As I was leaving, I passed by our church's library. I can't explain it, but a book just seemed to jump off the shelf. Written by Catherine Marshall, it was entitled *Adventures in Prayer*. The cover was oldish looking and melodramatic. I'd never read anything by Catherine Marshall. I always thought her more of a novelist, and I wasn't a big fiction reader. I was more into stuff by God or Dave Barry. But the pull of that book was so strong, I took it in my hand and prayed, "God, I have no idea why You want me to read this book, but I will, just because You're urging me to."

I took it home and read it in one sitting. It was an amazing little book filled with hope and inspiration. The author believed just as I did about the power of prayer, faith and God's sovereignty. I went on the website of the book's publisher, Chosen Books. At God's leading, I contacted the editor listed there, Jane Campbell. I called her "Miss Jane." I told her what my husband and I were up against. I sent her a weird string of writings from my "disaster journal," as I called it.

Miss Jane was so kind, so wise, so completely perceptive. She drew this story out of this dark period of our lives with such gentleness and understanding. I know God handpicked her for me not only as an editor, but as a trusted friend. She introduced me to warm, softhearted Trish, who edited my manuscript delicately. I so appreciated that, because I am the kind of person who shrivels like dried boogers when there is the smallest hint of harshness.

Thank you to our dear families. Thanks to Ridgeview Christian Church, to Greentree Christian Church and to the hundreds of people who have offered prayers, money, hankies, service and time over these past three years.

Jim Huskey, a family friend, has been so sweet and generous that if I ever once say something like, "Wow, I like your broccoli salad," he will start making it for me every other day forever or until one of us dies.

On more than one occasion I've said, "I couldn't last a minute without the Lord, but I don't think I could go a week without Kenny Salts, my brother Dan or Irene Troutt." They look after us in every way. The Jeffers family prays for us regularly and calls to ask, "What's for pizza tonight?"

And I could never forget to acknowledge my favorite teacher, Mr. Schantz. He made me promise to nurture my writing pencil as well as my paintbrush.

Above all, it goes without saying that every single non-evil thing I do or hope to be is for and because of Jesus Christ, my Lord!

I

On the Skids

It was the King Kong of bad days, one that would define many to follow. Lying in a grassy ditch and staring at the sun-bleached sky with my husband might have been romantic, except we'd just been thrown from a motorcycle. Allen was paralyzed, and I was struck silly. But I'm getting ahead of myself. Let me start at the beginning.

Our daughter, Lily, was three, and we'd been enjoying the best summer ever. Allen was a campus minister, so his summer schedule was flexible. He and Lily would spend afternoons together in the tiny vinyl pool on the deck. He was such a great dad, and he gladly kept her occupied while I worked from home as a freelance illustrator. I had just received great news from my agent that I was being assigned a series of children's books for a company I had long respected. When she told me the news, I screamed in delight on the phone, but no one was alarmed by my shrieks. No one scrambled to see if there was an intruder with a pickax in the house. "You scream and squeal a lot," people would tell me, so everyone knew that my screams were almost always happy ones.

Our wedding anniversary was always a signal that the college students were rushing back to the town of Rolla, Missouri, and things were hopping again. As Allen began spending more time on campus at Missouri S&T (Missouri University of Science and Technology), our anniversary always got pushed aside somehow in all the busyness, which made my eyebrows furrow and my face grump up. Late on our thirteenth anniversary, after I had spent a long day of chasing after a preschooler, tending to a messy house and longing for some adult companionship, Allen was nowhere to be found. I tried his cell phone, but there was no answer. It was 10:00 P.M., then 11:00, and my annoyance turned to worry. I tried the cell phone again—no answer. I did a lot of stewing, the extremely female type. Then I did what any girl in my position would do—I ate a bunch of granola bars and distracted myself with online shoe shopping.

Finally, the garage door opened and Allen came in, sweaty and grass stained, smiling from ear to ear. I hit him with a machine-gun torrent of estrogen-fed angst, and he apologized profusely. He had been out playing Ultimate Frisbee with a bunch of college guys. He loved that game so much! Everyone referred to him as the "Old Man," with a kind of reverent veneration. Even though Allen would never tell you so, the patriarch often gave those younger boys a schooling in how to play! In retrospect, I would come to regret my pettiness and be glad Allen had played that night. I didn't know then that it was his last time.

In part to appease me, we set aside another day two days later to celebrate the anniversary we'd missed. That one turned out to be a beautiful morning, the perfect backdrop to hang any memory on. Allen dropped Lils off for her second day of preschool at 8:30 and then rushed home.

"What do you want to do?" I asked enthusiastically as he bounded through the door. I was wiping up a mess of crumbs around the toaster. "Racquetball?" I suggested.

I am slight, nonaggressive, uncompetitive and nonathletic. Allen had to invent new ways to keep our games challenging enough for him—playing with his left hand, standing in one place the whole game . . . So he responded to my idea in a sort of *phone* voice, the one usually reserved for scheduling and/or schmoozing: "I don't have time for the gym this morning. I have a meeting at the office in half an hour."

I was disappointed that he was already reneging on our date, but I let it go. He kept busy and worked hard. We decided to make the best of it and take the motorcycle out for a quick joyride. It seemed like a year since we'd been on it together, and we had just enough time before his meeting.

Years earlier, when he first proposed the idea of getting a motorcycle, I objected. I thought I would never ride on it. But Allen was cautious, a very safe driver. We took things slowly and hardly ever went more than five or ten miles out of city limits. I came to love the wind in my face on our quiet rides through the countryside.

"Don't crash!" I teased as we got on. "It's our anniversary ride!"

"Like I'd ever crash on purpose," he sassed back.

We joked about whether or not our thirteenth anniversary on the thirteenth of August was something menacing, as the superstitious might suppose. The bike gurgled and chugged, not wanting to start at first, and I held my breath until we finally heard the engine turn over. Then we headed out toward our favorite country road.

I always thought about God when we rode, and I rehearsed Scriptures and hummed. I like to hum. But this particular morning was different. We hadn't been on the bike more than five minutes when I began feeling really nervous. We weren't in any perceivable danger, weren't going more than about 25 miles per hour, but I found myself praying a prayer I would think about over and over in the months that followed: "God, I don't like living fearfully, and I don't think it pleases You. So right here and now, I want to affirm my trust in You—I trust You to protect me and keep me safe."

Moments later, our motorcycle hit a patch of loose gravel left in heaps amongst some unmarked construction. We went off the road toward the ditch and were thrown twenty feet through the air.

"Chrissy," Allen asked after we landed, "are you okay?"

"Yes," I replied.

"I love you," he said.

"I love you, too" I answered. Even though I said the words, I have no memory of them. My mind was idling.

Allen filled in the details for me later. He had never lost consciousness and immediately realized our situation was dire. "Lord, please send someone to find us," he prayed.

In less than a minute, Rachel, a girl in our campus fellowship who was on her way to work, spotted us. The first one to see us, she called the paramedics and stayed on her knees close to my head, shielding my eyes from the sun. I had sustained a concussion and was determined "severely loopy."

Meanwhile, Tara, a pretty college student, waited outside Allen's locked office door in the campus house. She was to meet him at 9:00 that morning. They had a lot to get ready for; it was the opening week of classes after a long, lazy summer. They would plan activities for every night of the week to entice coming college students to get plugged in to a Christian ministry before their faith was bombarded by the allures of college life.

I imagine that Tara got fidgety as Allen went from a few minutes late to annoyingly late. I wonder if she thought, *Maybe he's on the FBI's Ten Most Wanted list and I never really knew him. . . .*

For the rest of the world, life was passing by on a normal Wednesday morning. People were checking in at work, running errands or wondering what to do now that their little ones were back to school. Up until this very moment, my life had ticked along just as predictably, and not at all soap-opera-ish. There was no all-out drama, no dumping beverages on each other in a heated quarrel. No hanging by my fingertips from a cliff while wearing a cocktail gown and stilettos as my life passed in front of my eyes to the tune of a softsational, one-hit wonder. Not even any childhood angst or teenage rebellion. No sibling rivalry. No tortured regrets other than a bad mullet and some poor fashion choices in the eighties. (But who doesn't regret the eighties, tight-rolled pants and multiple pairs of brightly colored socks worn all at once?)

In a sterile emergency room, my shell-shocked, groggy mind finally began to wake up, and I realized at once that I'd been catapulted into the realm of a serial drama. Nurses wheeled Allen into my room on a gurney. I was sitting on the table in a gaping hospital gown. (When they keep you for "observation," they mean it in every sense of the word!)

"Touch him here," the nurse urged, so I touched his collarbone.

"I can feel that," Allen said.

He was about to be taken by Life Flight to the university hospital two hours away. He had broken his neck, injuring his spinal cord at a high level.

Someone had picked Lily up at preschool and put her into my arms on the long, tall table in the bright white room with graphic anatomy posters on the wall. I tried desperately to make sense of what was going on. The most tragic thing in my life so far had been wearing Chic jeans when it wasn't chic and burying my pet hamsters, Nibbles and Waddles, so I just kind of thought everything would turn out okay since things usually went pretty well for us.

The emergency room doctors, however, were painting a different picture. They weren't sure Allen would survive. And if he did, they warned, he might not be able to move or breathe on his own.

A nurse came in with a phone. "Your mom is on the line," she said.

Oh no, I thought. *Everyone will be worried.* I was embarrassed about causing such a ruckus. Embarrassment seems a weird thing to feel in such a situation, but I just couldn't think properly yet.

I was released a few hours later. I had a terrible headache and a big strawberry on my hip. I threw up a couple of times in front of people. That was humbling. Otherwise I was fine, and a couple of friends drove me two hours up to Columbia, Missouri, where Allen had been transported.

I can't remember much about those first few days, just snatches. I remember waking in the middle of the night in a hospital waiting room and seeing my brothers sleeping on the rock-hard floor. I felt bad for them since I was in a semi-almost-practically comfortable chair. I remember Allen was on a table that tilted back and forth constantly, and he had a halo screwed into his head. His room was so hot, and we were so confused.

What seemed like hundreds of friends were visiting, hugging, stuffing cash into my hands. I felt lost. Mom gently scolded me when she found almost $500 I had just set down on a coffee table in the hospital waiting room. I had walked away from it, distracted.

A night guard on duty introduced himself a day or two later and handed me a Ziploc bag of Allen's things—his wallet, his wedding band, a garage door remote he'd put in his pocket for our return trip home, which had never happened. And his watch. The watch was all scuffed up and broken, the time gibberish. My natural tendency was to toss it in a wastebasket, and then I quickly realized it was not just a junked-up doodad. It was something of a relic. That watch had been so important. I remembered tiny Lily, barely talking, turning her daddy's arm to look at the face of it and saying, "Time to go," a comment she heard Daddy say so often. He was always on the move, and she had picked up on that even at such a young age. I gave the baggie a place of importance in my oversized purse that I carried everywhere I went. The purse had a big, fun owl sewn on the outside, which now seemed strangely inappropriate in our sobering surroundings.

In the weeks leading up to the accident, I had had trouble sleeping. I woke up almost every night at 3:00 or 4:00 A.M., unable to trail back off to sleep. So I'd drag myself out of bed, tuck my Bible under my arm like a football and find a quiet corner where I would talk with God. I'm glad we had that squint-eyed time together, He and I, because things soon would be turned upside down between us.

Likewise, when I prayed and affirmed my faith in God on the motorcycle that morning, I had no idea my faith would be tested so soon.

Are we still friends, God? Or am I on Your poop list? I wondered after the accident. Ever aware that His mercy is our only real hope, I found myself praying over and over, "Please be real, please be real, please be real!"

2

GROANS AND GRIMACES

I'm convinced that at least once in life, every person
finds himself or herself staring eyeball-to-eyeball with that one
big question, "Am I right about God?" I was born and raised in
church. I was Bible college–trained and had spent years in ministry. Yet here I was, back at the very foundation of it all, praying,
"Please be real!" Even though I was utterly, desperately dependent
on God more now than ever before, doubts still nagged at me as
Allen began what would be a three-week stay in the ICU.

Family was around much of the time to help look after Lily,
and we all pretty much lived at the hospital. Allen and I scarcely
had a moment alone together. Since I had a serious concussion,
the doctors ordered that someone stay with me all the time and
scoot me around in a wheelchair, which I constantly wriggled out

of and complained about. It was days before my mind completely cleared.

The doctors had surgically fused Allen's fourth and fifth vertebrae, and his situation became more critical than it was initially—blood clots, pulmonary embolisms, pneumonia, collapsed lungs. He still wasn't moving or feeling anything. Yet he was robotic in his even-tempered calm.

Finally, doctors gathered both of our families into a tiny room to tell us the news. It fell off their lips so easily that they surely must have rehearsed it. Allen's spinal cord was badly damaged at the C4 level, which meant he had no feeling or movement below his shoulders and his breathing was compromised. Time would tell what functioning would come back, if any. They didn't think any would. They quoted dismal statistics and gave us sober warnings. My mom looked faint. I was relieved that I had a head injury and wasn't expected to understand it all.

When Allen had roused after surgery, I slunk into his room and sat in the straight-backed chair by his bedside, skootched down in my usual slumpy posture. *He* was more coherent than I was. My knee was bouncing up and down nervously, as it always does in church or whenever I try to sit especially still. After a pause, I moved in close and said something dumb like, "Honey, promise me you're going to be okay, because I will believe you, whatever you say."

Even now, our dynamics had not changed. I was looking for him to take the lead and fix things. Almost excessively responsible by nature, he had been paying social security taxes since his adolescence. I think he viewed himself as stuffy and serious, even though he really wasn't. He liked it that I had some kid left in me. He beamed when he bragged to others that I was imaginative and fun. I would blush on cue. He made every painstaking effort to shelter my perceived innocence, making sure I wasn't bogged down with bill paying or anything having to do with lawn mowers or property taxes. He even helped with the menial things like sucking dead spider bits out of the corners of the windowsills with the vacuum and washing heaps of dirty laundry.

My mind wandered, a slideshow of carefree moments passing through my thoughts. Lils and I dancing around in a late-night summer rain. Drawing a curly mustache on the cat with a permanent marker for laughs. Riding an air mattress down our basement stairs—we called our ride the "Extreminator." It was more fun with a name.

Now I felt the weight of two worlds—this medical world of life and death, huge and all eclipsing, that forced us to ask, "Are we ready for eternity?" Then the regular world of stuff that didn't matter by comparison, but that I would have to address at some point—like the overfull trash bucket at home that I needed to squash down with my foot three or four times until it finally wouldn't go down anymore.

People called almost constantly to inquire about Allen's condition. It became laughable—one afternoon I was on the cell phone updating our pastor, a second cell phone was ringing in my bag (a phone my family had supplied to field their calls) and the lobby phone rang for me simultaneously. Everyone was hoping the doctors' reports would prove wrong, or that God would take His big, awesome mistake eraser and rub this whole mess up like a spill.

One morning I was riding in a car with my sister-in-law, Twila, heading back toward the hospital. We'd gone to a store to pick up some necessities: toothpaste, deodorant, chocolate. Allen's sister was blond, smart and gorgeous by anyone's standards. She was someone so enviable, so chock-full of talent and charm that you might be jealous, thinking she surely pulled the world along by a string. But in reality, she had been through so much—including a painful divorce. It had only made her stronger, more compassionate.

I confessed to her how hurt I was by God's silence. I felt dumped, forgotten, disappointed. I had loved God for as long as I could remember. I had hotly pursued Him. Now this? It was like He wasn't keeping up His end of things, even though I knew on some level that such a rationale was totally terrible.

"I'd just like to hear from Him," I told Twila as I reached for the phone ringing again in my purse. "Maybe that's Him now," I joked, trying to be wry.

My fun-loving, jovial sister, Deb, was on the other end.

"Are you a prophet of the Most High God?" I asked.

"No," she said, in an unusually serious way, "but I did feel God urging me to call you with this verse in Isaiah." She went on to read, "Can a mother forget the baby at her breast . . . ? Though she may forget, I will not forget you! See, I have engraved you on the palms of my hands" (Isaiah 49:15–16).

In response, I blubbered to her all about my torment and God's silence.

"A teacher doesn't talk while the test is being given," Deb comforted me.

I suppose I should have recognized at once God's love stamped all over those early days: the hand shading my face from the sun; the money lovingly tucked into my hands and purse by concerned church family; friends and relatives traveling from far away to comfort and hug on us and sleep on hospital floors. But I confess, that awful churning question, *Where are You, God?* was drowning everything else out.

Sometimes I do that thing you aren't supposed to do, where you flip your Bible open and then think the page it flops open to is somehow utterly significant. I can't help myself—I want to think God is up there, desperate for each of us to know Him in real, tangible ways. I want to think that He goes to great lengths to communicate with us in ways that are relevant to our here and now when we seek Him. So in the ICU waiting room, in a curiously quiet moment, I cried out to Him, "You could have prevented this, Lord. Why didn't You? I thought we were friends."

I hoped He would speak to me in some profound way, like coming down and knocking on the door, turning down His glowingness so I wouldn't be altogether terrified, and explaining things to me. (To date this has not yet happened, unless He was in disguise, selling fund-raiser cards or Rainbow vacuums or running for public office.) I opened up my Bible, sure He would speak to me through whatever passage my eyes fell on. I was a little disappointed when it opened to the story of Lazarus, so familiar that I was sure it had nothing new to offer.

Still, holding true to my magic-eight-ball Bible-reading technique, I gave it a shake. The girls, Mary and Martha, some of Jesus' best friends, send word that their brother is gravely ill. But instead of coming to help and heal, Jesus takes His time, helping crowds of strangers and poking along. By the time He shows up, Lazarus is long dead, four days and counting.

Jesus approaches the outskirts of town. Martha comes to meet Him, but Mary is suspiciously absent. She has a 'tude. My 'tude. Jesus immediately picks up on her intentional slighting, but He isn't upset by it. Instead, He asks for her. "Get Mary," He says as He patiently waits at the edge of town.

Of course, she comes running, as any of us would when God in the form of a BFF calls for us by name. "Hey, if You'd have been here, my brother wouldn't have died," she complains.

Jesus sees her pain and weeps. In a tag-team effort, Martha chirps in at the tomb with almost predictable annoyance: "Yeah,

yeah, Lord, we know our brother will live again at the big resurrection thingy."

To which Jesus replies, "Didn't I tell you that if you just believe, you will see the glory of God!"

Then, voilà! Dead man walking!

As it turns out, it was a pretty good little story to read while feeling at odds with my Maker, wondering why He just doesn't show up already.

Jesus had good reason for His delay en route to Bethany. Because Lazarus was dead and gone, you can imagine the stir when folks started bumping into him days later at the cappuccino bar. In fact, John tells us the very crowd that gathered to welcome Jesus into Jerusalem at His triumphal entry showed up because Lazarus was raised from the dead (see John 12:17–18). Prophecy was fulfilled, and Jesus received overdue glory because Mary and Martha held on through sadness and questions for a few days. Because they stuck with their Savior through disappointment, they played a key role in something of eternal significance.

I tried to hold on, too, and prayed something like, "God, I can't feel the earth spinning because I am so small on it. Maybe You are doing something big here, and I can't feel it for the same reason— my smallness, I mean. I'm trying to trust You. But sometimes it feels as though You are busy with other things—the Middle East, famine-type stuff. All way more important than a little family of three in the Ozarks. But I am hoping so hard that You care about all this and will help us . . ."

The doctors seemed so grim, and the halls and rooms of the ICU were such a dark, dark place in every way. Yet Allen managed to stay upbeat.

"I'm not going anyplace," he reassured me, and he meant it in a good way.

He seemed intent on beating whatever odds the doctors pronounced. Who knows, maybe he was just putting on a convincingly brave face to help all of us cope. He's like that.

My best friend from college came into the room. We all called her Frank, and she was surprised by Allen's easy smile and calmness.

"I'll bet your mom warned you about motorcycles," Allen joked with her. "I didn't stick my landing."

Looking back, I think our ignorance made the situation more bearable. We weren't really able to process what was going on. And we just kept trudging along, like the assembly line worker who somehow performs the same weary, monotonous tasks thousands of times without thinking too much about it. We readjusted to the sights and sounds of the new world we were in—a stark hospital room, unfriendly halls, an intimidating nursing station.

My days were spent at Allen's bedside during visiting hours, updating his visitors on the daily happenings, hugging old friends and family who traveled long distances to comfort us and chasing after our busy and extremely bored three-year-old girl. Having already pushed my illustration deadlines to razor-thin limits, I'd spend nighttime hours working late on sketches in the corridors of the hospital.

There were other people staying overnight in the hospital, too, waiting to hear news about their loved ones. I would study them and try to imagine what kind of horrors they were facing. My mother-in-law was especially good at reaching out to them, but I didn't get much past a goofy smile. When I could no longer deny that it was bedtime, I'd make whatever kind of bed I could in the waiting room and settle into it uncomfortably. Half-afraid to close my eyes, I struggled to figure out where God was in the middle of all this mess.

3

STALE CRACKER
PHILOSOPHY

One of the lowest points for us came when all kinds of tubes were stuffed into Allen, making him look like something from a mad scientist's lab. He was now on a ventilator, and a feeding tube went in his nose and down the back of his throat, right into his stomach.

It was humbling for both of us to find ourselves completely dependent on total strangers, nursing and hospital staff who were simple, everyday folks we might not have noticed before or thought of as a big deal. Yet now they were like presidents and kings. Their every unexpected kindness meant so much, like the nurse who brought in contraband ice chips to wet Allen's dry mouth.

Since they didn't know whether or not he could swallow, water and food were forbidden except through tubes.

On the rare occasions that he slept, Allen found himself dreaming of mouth-watering food. In fact, one night he dreamed that George Foreman himself had grilled up some steaks for him. Shortly afterward, he woke up to find a three-hundred-pound, muscle-bound linebacker in his room! It wasn't George, just a tech they called Little Joe.

The doctors decided there wasn't any hope of Allen getting away from the ventilator and feeding tube, so they scheduled surgery to have the feed line put right into his stomach. They seemed so cavalier and self-assured. It was a struggle to like them the way that I should have, and it really wasn't their fault. Allen couldn't even protest when they barreled in with their treatment plan. His voice was just a whisper, gone from the tracheotomy procedure.

I'm a people pleaser by nature, an avoider of conflict. I felt uncomfortable speaking up, but I insisted that the doctors try a swallow test. Allen passed with flying colors! By God's grace, Allen was off both the ventilator and the feeding tube in just a couple of days! Finally, a small victory! Our church family and friends rejoiced with us, and we felt a resurgence of hope. We were optimistic that we were making progress and that things were finally going in the right direction. The e-mail chains were all abuzz with the good report.

Allen was moved from the ICU to a step-down unit, which is the care level between an ICU and a normal in-patient hospital room. There, he finally got to see Lily again. It had been weeks since he had seen her. "I'm starting to forget what she looks like," he had soberly confessed.

Lily was apprehensive as we walked into her daddy's room. I wasn't sure how to prepare her. Somehow she knew everything was wrong, even without really being told. How do you explain this situation to a three-year-old child? I wasn't ready to say, "Daddy can't hug you anymore, or tickle you or bounce you on his knee. He may never hold you again, toss you in the air or carry you on his shoulders the way you love, way up high."

Allen was wearing all kinds of clunky stuff when Lily came in—a neck brace, IV tubes, weird boots and arm contraptions to keep everything just so. She barely spoke, but as soon as she realized she could feed Daddy and comb his hair, things picked up from there. The marker boards in his room, usually reserved for nursing instructions and medical terms, were soon decorated with simply drawn cat and dog heads, stick people and Lily's name in giant bubble letters. Twila also covered his bulletin board with family pictures and brought in fun, funky decorations to boost his spirits.

My brother Dave's family offered to take Lily back to our hometown of Rolla, Missouri, for a week so she could attend preschool and play with her cousins. Even though I hated being apart, I knew it was for the best. It would allow me to be more attentive to Allen and to field the steady stream of visitors who were stopping through. Everyone wanted to help, to do *something*. Some brought coolers full of snacks and drinks. A growing mountain of cards formed on the windowsill.

A lot of people were telling us things like, "Wow, you are so strong." Loosely translated, that meant, "Your life is really, really bad. And you keep on breathing, eating sandwiches, paying the gas bill . . ." (which was no small accomplishment).

Many well-meaning friends would pray with us, too, something like, "God, if it is Your will, if You would just say the word, Allen would be well!"

I would grin and nod demurely because I am the kind of person who smiles convincingly, even if you just said something that diced my heart to confetti. But inside, my reaction was, *Wow, do you really think God wants us suffering this way? Because that makes Him seem, well, not very nice.*

Mostly, I had attended churches that prayed earnestly for healings but got very nervous about whether or not people are actually healed these days. I wasn't always sure just why we prayed. For every promise I could think of in the Bible, I could recall the face of someone much worthier than I was who had finally succumbed to whatever crisis they battled. But how could we in good conscience say, "The Bible is infallible, the inspired Word of God," while at the same time explaining away the truth of its healing promises with slick technicalities when it didn't altogether match our doctrine or experience? I didn't have an answer.

Eventually, I got ready to make my first trip back to Rolla since the accident. I greatly needed to catch up on laundry, pack some fresh clothes and sort mail. And I was desperate to see Lily again. Before heading out, I sat by Allen's bedside. Even though his mom and sisters were there to stay with him, I felt terrible leaving. And I knew he hated to see me go. I had never actually seen him cry before, even when his dad had died a few years earlier. But he confessed to me then and there how badly his tears burned from all the medicine that was in his system. He also said that he had been embarrassed the night before because he couldn't wipe away his tears when a nurse had come into his room.

It all gave me that awful, stabbing feeling that hurts your chest in a physical way, even when you don't have an actual thing gouged in there. I moved in as close as I could to him with all the contraptions around.

I've noticed that in situations where I don't know what to say, I unintentionally turn Bibley. I'm pretty sure this comes off as really

annoying. In this situation, I said something to Allen about Saul/
Paul, whom God commissioned by way of blinding him.

"God has something big in store for you," I blurted out, trying
to sound convincing. Then I opened my tattered Bible and read
him one of my favorite stories about King Hezekiah.

At first the king was being bullied by Sennacharib, whose army
was causing a rumpus all around Israel. Sennacharib and his men
were known for being especially cruel. He warned Hezekiah at
high volume for all to hear, "Don't think that this God of yours
will save you."

Shaken, Hezekiah got on his knees and begged for God's help
and intervention. God rescued Hezekiah and his people, while
Sennacharib was killed at the hand of his own sons while worship-
ing false gods. But shortly after the triumph, Hezekiah became
deathly ill.

God sent Isaiah to tell the king the glum news: "Get your af-
fairs in order."

Hezekiah again despaired before the Lord, pleading his case.
God responded by adding fifteen years to his life. To prove He
meant business, God reversed the shadow on the sundial (the
preferred timepiece of the day) ten steps.

After I read the story of Hezekiah's healing, Allen and I prayed
together and said our sappy good-byes. The two-hour trip between
Columbia and Rolla was a familiar one, and the car seemed to
glide as if on autopilot. I came upon a storm front, and the skies
were almost black with menacing clouds. But from a small corner,
the sun shone through with laserlike intensity, right in the driver's
side window. God's warm love was so palpable to me.

A lumpy, thick glee came over me as I pulled into Rolla. For
so long there had been nothing but waiting rooms and cafeteria
food. I knew I was home when I first spotted a sixty-year-old guy

wearing jeans rolled up to his knees, combined with tall white socks and sandals. Then I read a sign in a hair studio window that said "Free mullet removal." It was so good to be home!

The house smelled and looked altogether new—familiar and comforting, but different—when I burst inside. I barely made it through the doorframe, burdened as I was with bulky shoulder bags and armfuls of stuff. Being home again was a huge comfort and relief, even though it was only for two days.

It seemed as though Lily had barely realized I'd been gone. She was having a good time with her cousins. Before the accident, we had never been apart even for a night. When we were reunited, I was all smiles. She promptly informed me that she had her life planned out. She would be a preacher/dogcatcher. She'd tell people about God, and if they didn't repent, she'd lock up their pets until they did.

"Sounds good," I said, with a grin and a nod. I was glad she had more direction for her life than I had for mine. I complimented her for being a good girl while I was away.

"Do I get anything for that?" she asked sincerely.

"Sure, babe, you've got all my love!" I said, taking her into my arms.

She was disappointed. "I thought I might get a toy or some sugar or money," she confessed.

"Nope," I said.

"Can I use the bathroom, then?" she asked.

"Um, yes," I nodded.

I was half-appalled at her rationale, wanting a toy for behaving well. Shouldn't my love and appreciation be enough? But at that moment I realized that I've always kind of approached God with similar expectations. I had really thought that trying hard to live in a God-pleasing way would translate into awesome stuff happening to us. But in reality, we don't always get what we want. And sometimes though we try our best, disruptive things happen—terrible things even. Yes, we have all His love, but we come off pretty disappointed when He doesn't come through with other stuff that we are practically desperate for.

Ooh, good analogy, I thought to myself, and I shuffled it away in my brain file to refer to later, in one of my churchy rants. I think I preferred the notion that God always prospers those He is pleased with, granting good health, wealth, success, amazing teeth. But so often it seemed the prophets, the disciples and even Jesus weren't embraced by life with open arms and a gift basket.

I got busy and dragged in a pillowcase full of stinking laundry. My brother's family left for Iowa, and the house became eerily quiet. For a while, I was overwhelmed with laundry and mail and the millions of other menial little things that were waiting for me. But then it started getting late. And creepy. I never even considered sleeping in our own bedroom. It seemed too blyucky. Instead, I took the easier route. I set up camp in a guest room and made Lily stay in there with me. When I finally fell into bed that night, I tried to imagine that Allen was just gone to camp, or on a mission trip with the college group. I wanted so badly for things to be normal again.

There were always those first few moments, when I would just wake up from a deep sleep, that I would forget our life was disastrous. Then the dark realization would sneak in that we were in the middle of something awful. I was glad this time, though, that I was home on a Sunday and I'd be able to worship with my church family again. I was homesick for them.

While getting ready that Sunday morning, I heard a strange and familiar beeping. A watch alarm. Allen's watch alarm. I retrieved it from my owl bag. The watch was working perfectly again, and even more strange, the alarm was set to go off at 8:43 A.M. each morning of the week. *Is there any significance to that?* I asked God.

I play the piano at our church. I play with a lot of gusto. I don't feel pompous saying that because I was always rather embarrassed about being good at it. I grew up wishing I played something cool like the bass guitar. Still, our worship team is a family. It was hard sitting in a pew and listening as they played without me, but it seemed every song that morning was just for me. The lyrics captured exactly what I wanted to say to God.

Then, while sitting there in our smallish, reddish, warm and loving church, it struck me that 8:43 A.M. was likely the time of the motorcycle accident that awful morning. It was called in at 8:50, moments after it happened. I kept the watch close at hand, and when it chirped on the hour, I thought about my prayer on the bike, a prayer that now seemed so puzzling. Sometimes, the thought of that prayer reminded me to keep hanging on. Other times, it needled me and made me wonder if that prayer slipped into black outer space or something. And then would come a gentle correction that seemed from heaven itself: "Whoa, girl, is that trust?"

One thing that brought me comfort in everything was trying to be faithful on my part—praying, trusting, hanging on to God with white-knuckled tenacity. It was like taking the burden of the outcome off my shoulders and putting it onto God's. The Bible says we should "always pray and not give up" (Luke 18:1). I kept praying.

God promised, "Those who hope in me will not be disappointed" (Isaiah 49:23). I *wanted* to keep hoping.

The Bible says, "Everything is possible for him who believes" (Mark 9:23). *Could I really ever believe enough?* I wondered. *Could I believe that much?*

If I do all He asks of me, I thought, *the burden is on Him to keep up His end of the deal, working it out for good. I know He can handle it.* And knowing that brought me unexpected relief.

It's a ticklish dilemma, how a wonderful, loving God can allow such awful things to happen. How I strained and struggled to understand it. I'm not sure a Bible college professor could even answer such an ugly question to anyone's satisfaction!

All too soon, my weekend at home was over and I was back at the hospital, sitting in the all-too-familiar waiting room. I felt refreshed by way of clean clothes and a hot shower, but I also came back with a newly injected dose of reality. I tried to work through a tidal wave of tough thoughts and questions as I tried to nail down just who was to blame—really to blame—for what we were going through. Not to blame for the bike spilling or the loose gravel left over from a construction mess, but for the evil in the world.

"I don't think it's God's will for anyone to suffer. That's just the thing the devil best loves, and how could God and the devil ever agree?" I blubbered to whatever pair of ears happened to be convenient at a particular moment. "If it isn't God's will for people to be well, isn't it wrong for us to try as hard as we can to get well? Wouldn't all our medical intervention be kind of a rebellion against His will?"

By the time I finished my ranting, my weary listener would be long gone, digging out change for a vending machine. Still trying to sort it out, I wondered to myself, *It's easy to recognize that not everything going on around this place is God's will. Why else would Jesus tell us to pray that God's will be done on earth as it is in heaven? So heaven gives us a better look at the will of God than the bad stuff that happens down here* . . . That thought spoke volumes to me about the character of God.

I thought about John 5:19, too, which says Jesus did exactly what He saw His Father doing. He did nothing but the will of God. And Hebrews 1:3, that Jesus was the exact representation of His Father. *Jesus would never zap someone with something like this,* I rationalized.

I opened my Bible and revisited the familiar story in Matthew 8:2–3 (NLT) about the leper who knelt before Jesus and pleaded, "Lord, if you are willing, you can heal me . . ." Jesus was heartsick at the very idea that He might not be willing—bone-deep, stomach-flipping, moved-with-pity heartsick at such a question. In one translation, Mark 1:41 even reads that Jesus was "indignant" when asked such a thing (TNIV). Fired up with emotion, He felt strongly about His answer—"I am willing!" Jesus touched him with His own bare hand without so much as flinching. The man was perfectly healed.

Can you imagine what a blast it must have been to travel with Jesus and the gang, celebrating with broken folks day after day who had been given their lives back? The miracles of Christ took on a whole new life to us as they now played out in our imaginations with new reality.

Somewhere along the line, I had bought into a chunk of bad and puzzling theology—that God sends sickness and calamity to teach us lessons. And when people are miraculously healed, it's fishy. Suspect. Now that I was in the middle of our situation, that rationale sounded a lot like the hokey religious leaders of Jesus' day, who scoffed that it was only by Beelzebub that this Jesus guy was doing miracles (see Matthew 12:24). The devil must love, *just love*, that thinking. It makes him smell like a rose, while God gets stuck stinking.

Another verse came to my mind, Hebrews 2:8: "In putting everything under him [Jesus], God left nothing that is not subject to him. Yet at present we do not see everything subject to him."

To me, that meant Jesus has authority over everything. *But it doesn't always feel that way,* I admitted to myself.

By this time, I was digging for change so I could solve the complexities of life over stale crackers and Fanta. I'm not one to talk to the devil, but his fingerprints were all over our mess. In a moment of hoity toity, I said to him, "I will not give up praying for victory. Somehow, God will use this to His glory. You will give up before I do."

But then it became all too obvious, before even a day had passed, that my resolve wasn't all that great. I wrote myself a paraphrase of Psalm 107:1 and kept it in my Bible as a reminder of what I knew to be true of God even when my feelings wavered: "Remember to tell God thanks for being so good. He is always so loving and kind."

4

THICK-AND-THIN HOPE

Allen still couldn't use his hands or walk or do other fun stuff like plate spinning or shadow puppets. And I continued to grimace toward God and question and wonder. I wondered if hope was something we can't really wrap our brains around until we are so scabbed up that we have nothing else to cling to.

God had prepared my Bible ahead of time. It looked like something kids get into trouble for, marked with highlighted verses He had led me to in the months leading up to all this. The verses all seemed to shout, *"Have confidence in God!"* And in their tone was that same patient forbearance that Jesus showed His disciples when He probably actually wanted nothing more than to clench His fists and teeth, squeeze His eyes tight and groan in frustration.

It seemed that almost every time I opened my Bible, I came upon Isaiah 30:18, "The LORD longs to be gracious to you; he rises to show you compassion. For the LORD is a God of justice. Blessed are all who wait for him!"

God had prepared my iPod, too. Nearly all the songs, with the exception of a few ABBA Gold and Bananarama essentials, had lyrics that would help to pull me through the long dreary halls of the hospital. (Actually, Bananarama helped some, too.)

We were so eager for Allen to be released from the hospital so he could move into rehab, where he could practice shrugging his shoulders a bunch. Unfortunately, that was still all of him that was moving. After numerous setbacks and delays, he was finally transferred. Slowly, he began to regain some movement in his arms. We had high hopes that with his athletic background, positive outlook and hard work ethic, he'd be running sprints in no time.

We thought that maybe you came out of rehab with all that you poured into it, but Allen's body just wasn't cooperating. Only a couple of hours in the day were actually spent doing anything physical. Much of the time was spent learning from the staff how to get along with whatever movement he had and addressing what we would need to know to live outside the walls of the hospital. At the time, that was frustrating to us because we only wanted to hear that he would recover.

By now, most of the family had gone home and visitors were a little more sporadic. A fellow campus ministry in Columbia put Lily and me up in their spare apartment. It was nice to have some space and a shower to keep the cooties at bay. We would spend days at the rehab hospital, where keeping Lily occupied was a constant challenge. I drew faces on rolls of medical tape, and she would play with them for a long time.

It seemed backward, but Allen looked better just hours after the accident than he did during rehab, as if he were getting worse, not better. Dear friends from college or wherever would reach out to us in sympathy and concern. They made every effort to juggle schedules and travel to visit us. It was pride, I know, but I didn't want them thinking our life was terrible.

It wasn't that I was afraid of being a "sissy-sissy, baby cry-pants." I'm not really sure why, actually, but I always found myself trying to put the best possible spin on things, the way you do with old gal pals or hairdressers or long-ago friends you reconnect with on Facebook, who knew you in braces and glasses so big that only about a fourth of your face showed.

It was like a mission trip I'd taken to Uganda. We'd visit people in their mud huts out in the bush. The huts were covered with thatch and painted with manure, yet decked out inside with doilies, magazine pictures taped to the walls and crude decorations. It seemed such a strange irony to me at the time, but now my life was like one of those huts. Even though no one would want to live there with us, I unintentionally found myself presenting things in the best way so that people wouldn't think our life was junk.

"We're really not doing anything more than what God asks us all to do—serve each other and trust Him," I'd say, ridiculously trying to sound wise and tough. But in the really truthy part of my heart, I had no idea why this had happened to us or how God could ever make good of it. Sometimes very late at night, in the college bunks Lily and I had pushed together in the campus house apartment, I felt very, very sad, and I hoped Lily wouldn't wake up and catch me wallowing in wet, slobbery self-pity.

One night, I woke from a sound sleep about 3:00 A.M. I didn't know why, but there was a word in my head and I had no idea what it meant. It was even like the word was spelled out for me, *ru-ha-ma*.

What on earth does that mean? I pondered. I knew I couldn't go back to sleep without writing it down. So I got up and typed it into a Google search right then, in the middle of the night. It was a Hebrew word that meant "compassion, one God loves and pities." I thought again about the verse in Isaiah that had been helping me so much—"The LORD longs to be gracious to you; he rises to show you compassion . . ." How often in the Gospels was the expression "Jesus had compassion on them" used? And it was always followed by Jesus acting on that compassion in some completely great way.

One way God had compassion on us was that Allen had a first-rate Christian doctor now, not just a little bit Christian—an all-out lover of God. They prayed together once a week. The Good Doctor had a crazy-wide smile, eccentric shoes, and he rode the bus everywhere. He always had new stories to tell about opportunities he found to share the Gospel.

Allen asked him pointedly if he had ever witnessed a real miracle, and he seemed to fidget uncomfortably. His response was something about a patient who had accepted his injury and gone on to become a recognized public speaker with a full life and a happy family. In short, the Good Doctor implied, the real miracle is when bad stuff happens but doesn't keep you down. Of course, he said it all more poetically.

Down deep, I think Allen was disappointed that his doctor's response hadn't gone the direction we'd have liked. Yet as far as recovery, Allen was doing better than average. A lot of people with his level of injury never regained any movement below their shoulders, but Allen was gaining good use of his biceps, and there was a glimmer of life in a few other arm muscles. Nothing in his triceps or hands, though. He was learning how to use a pencil snugly fitted in a wrist brace to poke buttons on a phone and computer. That would hugely enhance his quality of life and his ability to be left alone for short periods of time. Even though we should have been jumping up and down, ecstatic about these developments, it was hard not to wish for more.

Since Allen's car was more roadworthy than mine, I was driving it back and forth from the campus house apartment to the hospital. One afternoon, I came upon Allen's planner in its usual spot, just to the side of the driver's seat. How strange that this book, once a bona fide member of the family, was now completely meaningless. I flipped through the pages, an index card eerily stuck in the day, *that* day, to mark the place. Time had screeched to a standstill on that day, and all his appointments, once so dutifully kept, meant nothing.

Along with that, my illustration assignment that once had me captivated with my work was now like a dripping faucet—always reminding me of more I must do. I was still bogged down in the sketches phase and wondered how I would ever make my dead line, even though they had already given me generous extensions.

It became all too apparent that the world we usually live in isn't the real world at all. The things that we think mean so much mean nothing. *Maybe we were privileged to find this out before wasting a whole lifetime on nothing much?* I asked myself.

No, I decided, *there isn't anything advantageous in this situation.*

One morning when I left the apartment, it was pouring rain. Heading to the hospital, I was scurrying across the parking lot to the car with both luggage and Lily in tow. Desperately digging in my purse for the car keys, I kept grabbing the oddest things—a toothbrush, dirty socks, cracker bits. And then I felt a lumpy thing between the liner and the wall of my purse. The keyless remote to the car, lost for *two years*, had broken off my key ring and slipped through a tear in the purse's lining, into utter lostness—where it had waited for just such a day as this one.

I was so happy to find it, thinking I could at last get inside the car easily. Then I could continue the excavation of my overstuffed purse in a dry spot. When I used the remote to open the door, I heard the familiar ding you hear when the keys are in the ignition. I had locked my keys in the car, but was rescued by my unexpected find before realizing it! I guess there is something to be said for being in the right place at the right time. Dumbfounded by my happy coincidence, I backed into a retaining wall.

That's just the way things were going, one step forward, two steps back. Our world was becoming smaller. I felt guilty for every minute I spent outside the walls of the rehab hospital, and guilty for wanting to spend time away from it. It was a comfort to be in a room or restaurant where no one knew me and the only question I was asked was whether or not I wanted pickles. Aaaah. Pickles.

Still, we grew terribly fond of the familiar faces in the halls and lobby areas of Rusk Rehabilitation Center. Allen was making the most of his time there by sharing his faith with one boy in particular, a nurse's tech who helped him get dressed, get in and out of bed and such. He was one of our favorite people there, although if there hadn't been a dress code for employees, I might have been a little frightened of him. He had a tough exterior, but a lot of heart. Just the kind of person I think Jesus would have gravitated toward. I think that kid probably equated hope with "wishful thinking." He had been there long enough to see patients come in so sure they would walk out, and then leave with the same sort of predictable and sober outcomes that seemed in store for us. We never really knew what he thought about all Allen shared with him, but something in our situation made him at least curious.

It seemed as if with everything going on, we were missing the changing of seasons from summer to fall, my favorite time of year. And so every chance we got, we would sneak to an outside courtyard, where Lily would play with sidewalk chalk and Allen and I would just sit around, feel the sun and be close without dozens of other people around.

One night I was back home in Rolla to fax off sketches to my editor. It was late, and things felt especially bleak.

God, is it okay to hope? I asked. *To hope that Allen could be healed, I mean? And how long is too long? Is there a point when we should just stop hoping for more and accept things? God, I love You either way, and we'll serve You as best as we can either way. But I don't want to stop hoping. Just let me know*, I prayed.

I knew that people were sometimes healed. Occasional, modern-day miracles were undeniable. But there were so many people out there who were closer to God. Who deserved it more. Who needed it more. Was I a jerk to even hope for such a presumptuous thing?

Of all people, I should have grown up believing in prayer and miracles. The summer before I started fifth grade, my family took off for Washington, D.C., on our first big vacation. Behind our car we pulled a striped red, white and blue pop-up camper, and after a long, tough day of travel, we made it to Indiana. We were spending the night with family friends. Dad set up the camper right in their front yard. Mom and Dad slept on one side, my brothers on the other, and my sister and I in sleeping bags on the floor.

But in the middle of the night, I knew something was not right. My dad stumbled to his feet and said, "I'm sorry, sis," as he collapsed on top of me. My brother ran into the house and called 9-1-1.

Within moments, the yard was filled with red strobe lights and busy, cursing paramedics. Dad's temperature had dropped, and his blood pressure was so low that an EMT tossed a blood pressure cuff angrily aside. "This thing isn't working," he snapped, alongside some other unmentionable words.

My parents were rushed away, one by ambulance, one by police escort, while my siblings and I found ourselves being comforted in the middle of the night, in the middle of nowhere, by people we really didn't know well. I snuck into the couple's unfamiliar, peachy bathroom and hoped no one would find me. I got down on my knees and prayed for Dad, that God would give him back to us.

While doctors and nurses worked away, using paddles on Dad's chest and doing anything they could think of to get things going, Dad remembers hearing the devil throwing a tantrum when God insisted, "It is not his time—he is My child."

The next morning, doctors were baffled by Dad's recovery and even more confused by what had caused his spell in the first place. He was released that afternoon, and we all loaded up. Instead of going on to D.C., we headed back toward home without any remorse.

With no medical explanation for his attack or his mind-blowing recovery, Dad believed in miracles, too. One night, I was lying again in our guest bed, eyes wide open in the black room. Lily was snoring away, taking up about 90 percent of the queen-size bed, as only a preschooler can. Our portly cat was taking up another 5 percent, leaving me the splinter-sized edge. Just then, Mom called. It was late for her, after 11:00 P.M., but she wanted to tell me about Dad's dream.

In his dream, Allen was walking, which was nice to hear, but what got my attention was that she noted in great detail what Allen was wearing. That was strange. Dad doesn't really care about clothes unless they are covered with Bible verses or made out of donuts. (He is a big donut fan!) In his dream, Allen was wearing a puffy, red insulated vest. Dad took note since he'd never seen Allen wear anything like that before.

I had just ordered a vest matching that exact description for Allen a few days prior! The cold weather was coming on, and I couldn't figure out how to get a coat on him in the wheelchair. The vest actually arrived on our front step the morning after Mom's call. I headed back to Rusk Rehab full of hope. But for every moment of hopeful thinking, there were days on end of *ugh*. God never ceased to shine or to bless and warm us in unexpected ways. But it wasn't always on my terms.

Back in Columbia with Allen, I prayed one morning and asked that before the day ended, God would somehow give us some reason to hope. Morning and afternoon passed without incident. I popped a bag of popcorn in the activity room of the rehab hospital. It seemed a funny, ironic name, *activity* room, considering most of the patients it was intended for couldn't really move. It was strangely dark and quiet during these off hours, after having been abuzz with groups of patients all afternoon. There were puzzles and magazines (for guests) on unkempt shelves, and vending machines and couches that looked industrial and not at all homey. The soft pastel color scheme was a throwback to my high school days. I noticed the time flashing on the microwave. Evening was coming on. *Still nothing*, I mused.

Lily was away with family again (she had quite the social calendar now), so I slept on a chair in Allen's room that night, surrounded by the bleeping machines and creepy white walls that had become his existence. I didn't like spending nights in Allen's room, but I did so on occasion because I felt that since he didn't have any choice and always had to be there, I should be there, too. Traffic streamed in and out all through the night for this and that, and at dawn, a whole team of doctors would enter his room. And there I'd be, looking morningish. Yuck.

As I tried to drift off, I watched the minutes pass on the wall clock—11:52, 11:54, 11:58, 11:59 and finally midnight. I had felt no such assurance or hope from above all day. I struggled to know whether or not we were being "realistic" about things. Was that word in itself just a lack of faith in disguise?

"What is *hope*, anyway?" I grumpily pontificated as midnight came and went. It went beyond optimism, more than a thought or a wish. Right up there with *faith* and *love* in the "greatest of these" department, so I knew it must be good. I knew not to have it would be terrible.

Hardly a day passed when I wasn't somehow reminded that however bad I thought I had it, someone out there had it worse and was complaining a lot less. Right next to the Spinal Cord wing of the rehab hospital was a wing for severe brain injuries.

The truth was, I never even would have known that life was difficult if I hadn't experienced years upon years of God's blessing and favor from the time I was only up to someone's knees. Some people are just born into a big mess; they have no other point of reference. I had been blessed with a happy childhood. A loving family. A warm home. A full stomach and all that. And how many times I had prayed, *Jesus, You took my place. I deserved the cross; I deserved worse!*

Then this happened, and I turned like a two-sided coin in the air and told God, "Hey, what's the big deal here! I'm a decent person. I try to please You—what's going on?" I was probably scoring an F- in "Trusting God."

Eventually, even though I sometimes struggled with hanging on to my thick-and-thin hope, my thoughts would turn preachy again. And I would backpedal, as if trying to make peace with God. I wasn't sure where our lives were headed, but I was almost always praying, "Please be getting us somewhere."

5

GIVE-AND-TAKE

Lily was watching *Meet the Robinsons* on a portable DVD player in Allen's room at the rehab hospital. I hated letting her watch TV marathon style, but it was much easier there when she had something to do. The movie's premise was that a twelve-year-old orphan boy couldn't see the promise of his future because his present wasn't going well at all. It was based on a quote by Walt Disney, "Keep moving forward," and it was a poignant reminder to anyone up to their hair follicles in muck to keep going ahead, even if the steps are ugly and robotic at times, baby ant–sized even. I guess you can get a lot of good advice from people who are cartoon characters.

"Can we get me a brother or sister on the computer, Mom?" Lily asked earnestly.

"No, honey, you can't buy kids on the Internet," I replied.

"Oh," she nodded thoughtfully. "They don't like going in boxes?" she suggested.

I smiled and agreed.

I was losing track of how long we had been in rehab. Four weeks? Six weeks? Four weeks that felt like six weeks? Rehab had not been all we thought it would be. I was glad the staff was beginning to talk about setting a day for Allen to come home. But then there was that unabashed nagging in my mind, *Oh man, how are we ever going to do this?*

Allen still had no true sensation or movement in his hands or legs or trunk. According to the doctors, there was a limited window of time in which feeling and movement would return. Our days seemed to tick along like those annoying board game buzzers that startle you when they ring to say, "Time's up!"

Allen had initially been using a sip and puff chair controlled by a straw in his mouth. But now he had enough movement in his arms to crudely steer a joystick with his uncooperative hand. With the departure day fast approaching, therapists kicked in high gear, teaching us all they thought we'd need to know to exist at home.

Since Allen would be completely dependent on me for transfers, they taught me how to roll him around, get him in and out of bed and get him in the shower with a lift. They showed me how to stretch his arms and legs. Changing his clothes reminded me a little of dressing dolls as a child—except in a really non-fun way. The therapists and nurses made me promise to stop using the word *disaster* so much during our training. Weighing less than a hundred pounds myself, I thought the word *disaster* seemed fitting.

Up until now, I hadn't given much thought to how we would actually transport Allen back to Rolla or even get him in the house. We hadn't secured a handicap van yet, and our house wasn't accessible either. So late one night in the apartment, I began pricing vans and ramps online.

Lily was asleep. I had missed dinner and was craving almost anything. The little apartment we were staying in had no kitchen, and having been accosted there by a big, hairy spider days earlier, I didn't keep any food around to attract unwelcome guests. So with no munchies around to speak of, I ate eleven of Lily's gummy vitamins in one sitting. Eleven, for crying out loud!

"It's Friday, but Sunday is coming," a voice on the radio sang. I lost myself in the lyrics, singing along loudly until I feared Lily might wake up. It made me feel good to sing my heart out right there in the middle of our mess.

I soon felt a cold, sick fluttering in my gut, though, as I began to grapple with the practicalities of all we would need in the immediate future. I had no idea how we would ever manage the expenses. The price of handicap vans, lifts, ramps and equipment was outrageous! And like most people, we weren't wealthy, nor did we meet the guidelines to qualify for a lot of government assistance. It never entered my mind to ask anyone for help.

A glimpse of the news reminded me that there was life outside our tiny sphere. It had been a catastrophic week for Wall Street, and everyone was talking about the global economy crisis. There was talk of a $700 billion bailout bill to get things rolling again. In an interview, Fox News asked a congressman why $700 billion dollars specifically. He said, essentially, that no one knew how much would be needed to fix things, so they just picked a "really big number."

That's my kind of math, I chuckled to myself. *What they need is my mom in Washington, D.C. She would iron out the budget, and public officials wouldn't get away with half as much. And there is a higher-than-expected chance that most of them would lose car privileges,* I grinned.

This was a terrible time to have an expensive health crisis. There hadn't been any other time in my life when I felt so utterly dependent on God, even for our mere survival.

Our pastor called the next day to let me know that the board members at our campus house in Rolla had built a ramp to our front door. It was such a relief to me that they had just jumped in, instead of asking what they could do for us. I could never think of anything to say when people asked that, and I would lie by responding something such as, "We're fine, really. Is there anything *you* need?" I hated asking anyone to do anything.

We got some good advice about vans as well. We'd rent one to start. It was tricky to find one that didn't smash Allen's head when he rode his chair in and out of it, but we finally settled on one that worked well.

The evening before Allen's release, the doctors had us try a night in a small apartment room right on the floor of the hospital. It was there to give people one last "rehearsal" before they were completely on their own. It was a comfort to be just the two of us again, especially knowing that the nursing staff was right next door. Allen became very sick in the night. His fever spiked up around 104 degrees. *Good grief, I broke him already!* I worried.

On top of that, Allen also suffered from severe insomnia and I was up and down all night fielding his requests. I was completely exhausted by morning. I began to feel even more uneasy, wondering if I had the stamina to do this night after night, day in and day out—just me.

The doctor decided that Allen had an uncomplicated infection, prescribed some antibiotics and dismissed him from rehab on schedule so he could be home for Lily's fourth birthday. We would celebrate it with a welcome-home cake made by one of the doctors' wives.

It took longer than we expected to say our good-byes and load everything up, but friends came to help us make the trip home. We were so relieved to see them! As we drove away from the parking lot, a ball of nervous indigestion grew to boulder size in my stomach, as if I'd chased down a tub of fire-hot Thai food with a tumbler full of Tabasco sauce.

We snuck back into Rolla quietly. Friends made an effort not to overwhelm us. A few things were obvious at first glance. I'm not really fussy about the lawn. It could have tractor parts, chickens and grass growing heads of grain, and I would say something such as, "Can you believe that color of blue in the sky?" or "Did you ever see such a huge grasshopper?"

It's not that I'm totally obtuse about such things, but let's just say if I got a B-minus in courses like Operating a Leaf Blower 101, Advanced Lawn Mower Detailing or How to Keep a Meticulous Garage, I wouldn't call home with tears of regret. But even I noticed and could hardly believe our perfectly manicured yard and flower beds still exploding with blooms, even though it was October. With great graciousness, our dear neighbors had mowed, weeded and fertilized. And they continued on even when we protested.

"Let me do it . . ." I started in.

Pat interrupted me midstream. "We're Catholic. It's not just grace for us—we *have* to do nice stuff," he teased with a big smile. In the short time he and his wife had lived in Rolla, they had become stalwarts in their church and in our neighborhood.

One of the first people eager to greet us was our friend and neighbor Becky, a math kind of person who had offered to manage our bills while we were away. I was greatly relieved by this because under the best of circumstances, I am the Hurricane Hugo of checkbook ledgers. I have a terrible habit of writing the check number in the dollar amount spot and forgetting to record stuff.

And scribbling things into the margins. And doodling little shoes in parts of the ledger where they aren't appropriate.

In the past, Allen preferred that I not mess with the checkbook. He never understood how I could be so terrible at it. I would laugh at my mistakes when things came up, but my laughing about it kind of made him grumpier. Becky wasn't only saving our bank account, she may very well have been saving our marriage! She offered to help us a while longer, even though we were back in town.

"Good idea," chimed in Allen. "Otherwise one of us might kill the other," he laughed.

"I think I have the edge," I joked dryly.

Becky would write the checks to pay our bills and have me sign them. She knew things were tight. "You've got these monthly giving commitments; what should I do about them?" she asked.

I am so ashamed to admit that I paused before I answered. I didn't know just what we'd be doing for money, or if we could pay all our bills or exactly where tens of thousands of dollars for the electric wheelchair and van would come from.

When God asks us to give, it isn't because He needs a few bucks, I rationalized to myself. *It is an act of faith. An acknowledgment that, yes, I totally believe God is real and will take care of us. But will He really take care of us? Is it responsible to give this money away when I have no idea how we will meet expenses? Last time I trusted Him . . .* I gulped. I reasoned all this in that split second of silence.

"Keep paying them," I answered. And I am so glad I did. At that point, God poured out His provision in ways that were a little embarrassing. The board members at the campus ministry had taken out a generous disability insurance policy for Allen years prior, upgrading it just one month before the accident. And without even asking, our church opened a fund for the money that had begun pouring in to help us. Because of a typo, it was initially advertised as the *Schofield Family Fun* instead of *Fund*, and we were amused by the irony.

I hated taking a penny we hadn't earned from anyone, especially some of our dearest friends, but with everything we had to think about, it was an indescribable comfort to know that money would not be an additional stressor. We waited almost a year before gathering the courage to ask our church secretary for a list of people who had given money toward the fund. We had no idea how we would ever say thanks in a way that would match the gratitude we actually felt. And even after so long a wait, I could never have been prepared for the swell of emotions that came over me when I read the donors' names. Our dearest friends. Church family. People we didn't know who simply gave because they love God so much that it spills out over others.

The most humbling were those names of people who we knew scrimped and saved and lived much more meagerly than we did, in homes not as nice as ours, with cars not as nice. This would dramatically change the way we viewed money. We scrutinized every expenditure to make sure the gift money was spent on things that every person on the list would approve of and deem necessary. It brought to mind a whole new picture of stewardship and what it means to be stewards of the things God entrusts us with.

Consumed with guilt and conviction about all the excess in our lives, I said to Allen, "We need to go through our things, sort out the stuff we don't ever use and give it away to charity."

"Like what?" he replied. "The stove?"

I could always tell when he had impressed himself with a good zinger. He would never laugh outright, but the corners of his tight lips would turn up ever so slightly and the pockets under his eyes would bunch. My mouth gaped open in a shocked, fake-wounded way, and we laughed.

"Oh, go ahead and punch me as hard as you want," he urged. "Just keep it below the collarbone, okay?"

This injury had opened up to us a whole new world of jokes about ourselves that otherwise would have been in poor taste. They might still have been in poor taste, actually.

The churches in town had also taken into account my culinary shortcomings. They alternated, providing a meal almost every day of the week. In all our years of marriage, we had never eaten so well. Folks seemed to enjoy the friendly competition between churches.

"Who made the better pasta?" our preacher's wife asked.

Of course, I said hers was the best. She was so smart and classy and intimidating that I would have complimented her chunky fish ice cream, had she brought it. "Awesome texture, and what a wonderful blend of flavors," I would have bubbled robustly, with hand gestures to make it more believable.

Our church also had put together a prayer chain. People prayed for us around the clock every hour of the day, and most time slots had multiple people praying.

My kindhearted brothers and their families drove down whenever they could to build things, do projects and help with every single man-thing imaginable—ramps, vehicle stuff, computer problems.

When the cold weather came, there were shovelers. Every time it snowed, half a dozen people would come by wanting to help shovel. Most of the time it had already been done by someone in a mysterious white pickup truck. He would come sometimes at 1:00 A.M. to clean our driveway without being seen. We couldn't figure out who it was! Finally, we identified him. It was the husband of Lily's Sunday school teacher from church, never one to be a hotshot. What humbleness and hard work, with no thought of reward! I dread shoveling snow so much, if I had to pick between shoveling that driveway by myself in frigid cold temperatures or grinding my teeth down to nubs, it would take me very few minutes to decide that my teeth were history.

On Allen's first Sunday back at church, applause broke out at the sight of him, as if we were at a rock concert or the Super Bowl. I was back on the piano, overly conscientious about the goofy skirt I was wearing. I'd gotten it from a thrift shop, sort of dared into it when Lily taunted me, "Ugly skirt, Momma."

"Um, thanks, but I'm not taking fashion advice from someone who wears underwear on her head," I retorted.

Allen thought the skirt was Spanish looking. "Olé!" he had said coyly as we scooted out the door.

So there I sat uncomfortably in a very loud skirt, feeling very weird looking.

I saw my friend Maggie slinking in late. She was a beauty, fashionably dressed, wearing heels so high they looked like skewers you roast hot dogs on over a fire. She was the university's homecoming queen, dramatic and full of fun and mischief. When our eyes met, she changed her half-embarrassed, swift shuffle to find a seat into a theatrical fashion-model runway stride down the "catwalk" for laughs. I smiled broadly, and my tensions began to melt. She was *so* lovable.

As communion time approached, I started to panic, realizing that there was no one to serve Allen communion. I was at the front of the church, and he was all the way at the back. I felt terrible that I hadn't considered it ahead of time, and now it would be such an awkward thing. Since Allen still couldn't use his hands, he would have no way to get hold of the cracker or juice.

Then I noticed our minister, Dave, had positioned himself strangely out of place, at the back of the church. He usually sat on the front row. A dozen other things must have been on his mind, as he would be speaking in just minutes. But when the trays were passed, he moved in close and served Allen communion. I knew if Jesus promised a reward to anyone who gave a cup of water to someone in need, He must have something extra great for one who shares a communion cup. Dave did this for weeks, until other people jumped in. I loved how the guy leading our church was humbly serving in a way that perhaps no one else noticed.

Allen's therapy sessions at the local hospital dried up with insurance limitations, so people from our church and another one set up a schedule to come help him with physical therapy several times a week. This allowed me to catch up on some of the essentials around the house, like random quality control tests of my pillow, mattress and blankets. I had become exhausted just trying to keep my eyelashes above water.

Our entire church prayed for and cared for us continually. Every need was met before we even thought of it. Money poured in for the impossibly long list of resource-draining equipment and medical expenses. Among the prayer warriors, snow shovelers, food makers, van drivers and muscle movers, there was even someone willing to move the dirty sock left on our kitchen floor for no less than two weeks. People did all these things for us without being asked. I'm so glad they offered without waiting for me to figure out what we needed them to do. It made things so much easier, and we were overwhelmed with gratitude.

6

THE INVISIBLE HAND

I was still working on the children's book series I had agreed to illustrate just before the accident. All the while, I thought it weird that a job that once made me feel important, and an ambition that used to scream at a deafening decibel, turned out to be kind of nothing, an empty pursuit.

The only chance I had to work was after Lily and Allen were in bed. I would stay up every night until 1:00 or 2:00 A.M., be up several times after that with Allen, and be up early to get Lily off to preschool in the morning. I had wanted so badly to do my best illustrating work, but under the circumstances, I was relieved just to get something down on a page. Something that wasn't completely, tragically awful. Something that didn't go down in history as "Worst Ever." Something that wasn't so, so bad that the powers-that-be would confiscate my paintbrushes, pencils and computer just in case I had the gall to try again.

The lack of sleep and all the drama of our lives were wearing on me. My memory often failed me. One day, I was preheating the oven when I noticed a really weird smell. A *bad* smell. I opened the oven door and, to my horror, saw two raw hamburger patties that I had forgotten in there for more than ten days. I'm not sure which was worse, the raw, decomposing beef stinking up our house or the fact that I hadn't turned on my stove in over a week.

Another afternoon, I was carrying Lily into a grocery store. I picked up the pace when Lily announced that she needed a bathroom. My feet tangled over a curb, and we both went down. I toppled onto Lily in a gravel-filled median! The sharp rocks scraped up her back a bit, and I fussed over her in a melodramatic way.

In a twisted role reversal, Lily scolded me, embarrassed by the scene we were causing. "Just get *up*, Mom!" she said.

It seemed to me that in a single day, we had gone from being sometimes burned-out, overactive, helpful church leaders to becoming needy weaklings who could barely get through a day without relying on others. It seemed as if there were two categories in the family of God, Givers and Needers, and we were definitely in the latter category. In the not-too-distant past, we had found it sometimes awkward and draining to give. But now, needing all this extra attention was embarrassing and humbling. We were so grateful to be part of a church family in which people took care of one another.

It reminded me of the story of the sheep and the goats in Matthew 25. The passage is a reminder that one day we'll all come before God, and He'll ask us whether or not we've been merciful. It turns out in the end that those millions of silent "how you live your life" decisions we make every day without giving them much thought are a big deal!

In college, we had studied practice tests to make sure we were good and ready for the real test the next day. Here in Matthew, God had given us the big questions in advance so that we might face our biggest moment with confidence when we first meet Him and hear Him ask, "Did you *see* people? What did you *do* to comfort those in need?"

For the first time I could remember, we were the receivers in this passage, the puny "weakest of these" recipients of undeserved kindness. I could never list or repay all the small and large kindnesses that people were showing us, but I knew that no gesture of compassion they made would be forgotten by God. Compassion carries eternal dividends—the safest, smartest, surest investment possible.

Allen's sister, a missionary to New Guinea and Thailand, explained that overseas, asking for things is a crucial part of building relationships. "A friendship can never go to the next level without giving and taking," she said.

"That explains a lot about college roommates," I reminisced. Our girls' dormitory was a shoe and wardrobe free-for-all. A hair goop and face cream swap meet. There was plenty of give-and-take! One morning, a suite mate began spraying her complicated coif with an aerosol can she believed contained hairspray—only it was deodorant. Her flattened hair smelled fresh all day!

One quiet evening, Lily came to us bursting with exuberance. "Who wants to play Red Light/Green Light?" she asked.

Allen was engrossed in a baseball game. I was reading on the couch. There was silence.

A second request, as she tried to bribe us with candy she had stored in her "underpocket." (This was the supersecret pouch wedged just between her underpants and her little paddies. I choked back my laughter and tried to look disapproving.)

"Who wants to play Red Light/Green Light?" she asked more loudly.

Silence.

Lily does that thing most kids do, asking the same question with increasing volume until they get the desired answer. A third, *louder* request, "Daddy, you want to play Red Light/Green Light?"

"Sorry, I'm a quad," he smirked wryly.

"You can zoom in your chair," she said. "Mommy?"

Silence.

Sometimes we wanted to play and do kid stuff, but sometimes we didn't want to very much, or we were tired or had our own stuff we wanted to do. I guess I kind of assumed it was the same way with God—as if I were a nuisance coming to Him with every little request. Of course, I was pleading with Him about the biggie thing all the time—Allen's healing. But I tried to avoid troubling Him with the smaller stuff. I'd save up, and then when I reached a breaking point, I'd blurt out something ridiculous: "God, could You *please* do this thing for me? I will try not to ask for any more stuff again for a *really* long time"—as if God had to be bargained with.

My mom once told me that my brother's wife prayed before she went shopping at a garage sale that God would provide just what her family needed. They lived so frugally. Their entire family had an almost magical, unspoiled charm practically extinct these days. But I think at the time my mom mentioned it, I secretly thought, *Good grief, the prayer waves are getting gumbled up with garage sale requests? I've got huge quadriplegic prayer requests that need to get up there!* In time, God would show me how wrong my thinking was.

Lily was just beginning to read. She had her eye on a secret journal she wanted. You had to speak a password to get it to open. I told her it would be a reward when she learned to read. With that incentive, she practiced tirelessly, working hours at a time until she made her way through a big compilation of *Dick and Jane* stories and nine other small books.

Proud of her achievement, we gave Lily the journal as promised. But two days later, while I was back working with Allen, I heard her sobbing. The plastic latch that kept the journal tightly shut until you spoke the password had already broken. I tried every way imaginable to get it back in place, finally unscrewing the back, only to realize I could put my finger all the way through a hole where the latch belonged. There was no hope of fixing it, so I broke the news to Lily. She lay crying on her bed. I closed the journal back up and tried a few more times in vain to do something, anything.

I felt as though I should pray about it, but I felt soooo silly. I said something such as, "God, I'm embarrassed to ask about this; I don't think You're into this sort of thing. But still, could You . . ." And then I couldn't bring myself to go any further.

An idea came to me. I went online to see if the company made replacement parts. I found a cached page with dozens of replacements and felt hopeful. While my fingers flew over the keyboard, a visiting family member came to me with the journal in her hands. She said almost in a whisper, "I can't tell that there's anything wrong with this."

I took it in my hands, confused, and it was latched and shut tight. A piece of paper was hanging out the bottom, and I wondered if it might have tightened things up? But that didn't seem likely; I just couldn't make sense of it.

I called Lily because I didn't know the password. She spoke the password, the door opened and the blue plastic latch that had been completely missing just moments before was right there in place. The journal was as good as new!

I could not believe it. I stammered sheepishly, "I prayed about that."

"I did, too, Mom!" Lily exclaimed.

"I didn't know God cared about stuff like that," I said to Lily, still amazed.

In her simple, child's wisdom, she responded, "I guess God cares about what we care about."

A few days later, I was surprised when I read about King Asa in 2 Chronicles 16. King Asa started out strong, doing away with Judah's idolatry. But he didn't like asking God for help. He preferred to rely on human resources. That didn't go very well. Asa became ill but didn't seek God, only doctors, and he ended up dying of a killer case of athlete's foot. Reading between the lines, God must have thought, *Even when he felt terrible, Asa didn't bother asking Me for help. What was that guy thinking?*

God is mad when we don't ask Him for help? I questioned. *How can that be?* I was having a hard time believing that God really *does* like His children to come to Him for every little thing. I couldn't relate to that because I'm really—really—not that way.

For instance, my birthday came. I had turned thirtysomething a few times already. Call it a midlife crisis, but I asked for a pair of old-fashioned roller skates with pompoms on the toes. And since I was the one doing the birthday shopping, I got them. Lils and I raced around the block. She was on her bike. Old, lurchy, out-of-practice me on skates was struggling to keep up, with all the grace of C-3PO, the irritating droid from *Star Wars*. Halfway around the loop (which felt more like a trip around the world), at the farthest point from home, Lils said, "I'm thirsty, Mom. Can you go get me a drink?"

"Are you kidding me?" I panted. *"Noooo!"* I wailed in possibly the loudest voice I have ever actually used.

Even though she was my darling kiddo and I'd gladly give her a semi-vital organ or saw off my own limb for her in a pinch, I was slightly appalled that she would ask such a thing.

Later on, though, I opened my Bible to Isaiah 41:13, "I am the LORD, your God, who takes hold of your right hand and says to you, Do not fear; I will help you." Call it a hokey coincidence, but my right hand had been tingling for weeks, and I remembered an entry in my prayer journal I had written in the weeks after the accident. It read, *God, I wish I could feel my hand in Yours, the way a child holds her dad's hand in a street or a busy parking lot, when things could be dangerous and she needs extra looking after.*

If pressed, I would have admitted that God didn't miss a day or an opportunity to help us. He had provided for our every need through our families, our church and friends. He had kept us all very healthy, even through stress and lack of sleep, and even after doctors' warnings that Allen would most assuredly be at higher risk for complications and pneumonia.

In addition, even though Allen still wasn't able to walk or use his hands or stand or sit poker-straight on his own, he had enough mobility to be useful and modestly independent. He could use his computer with a pencil that he held in a brace fitting over his wrist and hand. With the pencil, he could operate a remote control and a phone. We used Velcro to attach them to a tray that fit on the wheelchair. Velcro became a staple at our house, so much so that I found two boxes I had mistakenly placed in our refrigerator.

"The silver lining in all this is that you're around a lot more to answer the phone," I joked to Allen. That was a job I hated so much it could be an event on the show *Fear Factor*, along with chugging a pail full of monkey entrails or kissing a leech. I considered them all equally repulsive.

With this new revelation in my heart, that God *wants* to help us, invites us to ask Him and is disappointed when we don't, I bombarded Him with requests almost constantly. I grumbled through tough days and sleep disturbances and used lots of caffeine, along with eyeball rolling and fake barfing/gagging noises when I had to do gross stuff like catheter changes, toenail clipping, booger rockets, zit popping, armpit hair trimming, flossing, ear hair shaving . . . A lot of grody maintenance was involved in measuring up to Allen's meticulous grooming standards. (To be funny, he sometimes referred to himself as "eye candy.")

"Help me face this, please," I would pray as I stumbled through periods of sleepless nights, exhausting days and yucko tasks. And even though I couldn't always feel God there beside me, I tried to believe it was so.

7

Still Calming Storms

I shuffled through Lily's backpack and came upon a book order form from Lily's preschool. It told the story of Dr. Seuss and stated, "Theodor Geisel wrote stories on a machine called a typewriter."

I found a weird sort of comical amusement in the statement, what with my background in champion typing and all. In high school, I actually participated in a nationwide typing contest. How nerdy is that?

"Typewriters are at least better than those newfangled Black-Berries. Who are those made for, anyway? People with tiny, little midget thumbs?" I joked, even though I knew Lily had no idea what I was talking about.

I had questioned whether or not to send Lily to a few hours of preschool a week, but now I was grateful for school. Lily adored her teachers and classmates, and it made her life seem a little more normal, I think. She was thriving there, but was always tuckered out by bedtime. I tossed her backpack aside and tried to make room for myself on her bed next to her, which meant moving about twenty stuffed animals.

"This is the best five minutes of my life," I beamed as our cheeks touched. "I could hug you the rest of my life and never get tired of it," I said, snuggling with her.

"I could hug you the rest of my life, too, except you're going to die a lot sooner than I am," she replied.

Lils had been putting her dad and me in our humble places with great aptitude ever since she came on the scene. I melted to goo the first time she said, "I love you, Mommy. I love you, Daddy." Then she added, "I love you, TV." We were instantly deflated.

She had already moved on in the conversation. "Where do baby kittens come from?" she asked earnestly.

I braced myself, sat tall and replied, "From momma and daddy cats."

"Do they have to lie down beside each other? Oh, never mind, this is getting gross." She shook her head, nose wrinkled in disgust.

I read her a Bible story and said, "Lils, promise me you'll always love God, okay?"

"Okay," she said. "Besides, it is pretty hard for me to turn bad. I'm just a kid, and I don't have any weapons or anything."

Before I could catch my breath, she returned to our previous train of thought. "Mommy, who *is* going to die first, me or you?"

To be honest, I had been so caught up in our own tumultuous tornado of emotions this past several months that I hadn't thought much about what Lily was feeling. She was young and resilient, I had thought, and she seemed to be handling everything so well. Now I reconsidered. *She must be worried about losing one or both of us*, I thought. I wanted to answer her question delicately.

"Well, honey," I stammered, "maybe we'll both go to heaven at the same time. Maybe the Lord will come back for us before anyone in our family dies . . ." I prattled.

She interrupted midstream. "Nope, you're definitely dying first," she said matter-of-factly. "I sure will miss you," she added.

"I'm planning on being around for a long time, baby. You'll probably be all grown up with children of your own before I die," I reassured her.

"But when your hair turns white and your teeth turn black," she cinched one eye, "you are about to die." She continued, "Dying of old age is the best way to go, I think, besides a sword." (She'd been learning about the Revolutionary War, but that made her statement no less terrifying.)

Allen rolled in just then to pray with us and do some smooching. We all prayed together, hands outstretched as best as we could. We offered our lives and every part of our bodies and strength to be used as God saw fit, even if the ways were scary or disappointing. Lily prayed that her daddy would be healed before she was too big to ride on his shoulders, and she promised to grow as slowly as she could.

I kissed her and tucked her in. Then I got Allen into bed, a long process that took over an hour.

"What time did you give me my meds?" he asked.

"Something something o'clock," I responded. I had no idea.

He rolled his eyes humorously as I pulled the blanket up to his chin. Somehow, we both understood that I was totally ill-equipped to be responsible for anyone's general well-being, yet here we were—a child, a paralyzed hubby, a half-starved beta fish and a meaner-than-average cat all depending on someone who once put on the same undergarment twice because she hadn't realized, *Hey, I just did that.*

When everyone was snug in bed, I buried my face on a rug in the living room. I prayed there on my knees every night and gave God the 411 on my life (as if He didn't already know). It was the only chance I had to do so. Every day was so completely crammed full of requests and responsibilities that these late-night rendezvous with God were absolutely essential. I was completely spent by the time I fell into bed.

But even sleep was interrupted. Allen suffered severe insomnia, and we were up and down half a dozen times one night, ten times the next. We were up for head scratchings, readjustments, pillow fluffings, gulps of water, deep thoughts, banana feedings, rolling overs.

"Should we get an algae eater?" Allen asked one time. "Could you write that down? And please, turn off the closet light." Then he would wake up the next morning and say something clever and endearing like, "I couldn't sleep. I just tossed and turned all night . . . my head, that is."

"Actually, I was the one tossing and turning you all night," I smarted back.

I would crawl in beside him sometimes to be close, and he would lovingly try to caress my back, but he had no idea how hard he was rubbing. It felt like he was rubbing my skin off with a cooking spoon, but I tried my dead-level best to make a face that said, "That feels awesome." Once, we laughed when we realized he had been mistakenly stroking his own leg!

The lack of sleep would sometimes get to him, and in that in-between stage, he would talk crazy.

Allen: "Honey?"

Me: "Yeah?"

Allen: "I love you."

Me: "I love you, too."

Allen: "You know that song from *How the Grinch Stole Christmas!* 'Wahoo Doray'?"

Me: "Um, yeah."

Allen: "Let's make that our song. Like if we are gone a while and come home, we could listen to it."

Me: "Okay."

About twenty minutes later . . .

Allen: "Honey?"

Me: "Yeah?"

Allen: "Do you still use Rogaine?"

Me: "Uh . . . no."

Allen: "Good, because that's what they used on the Vietnamese when they brought them over."

I've never used Rogaine, mind you, and I'm not sure what it has to do with the Vietnamese. But I made a mental note: no more History Channel for Allen before bed.

About twenty minutes later . . .

Allen: "Honey, was Brown Bear a good guy or a bad guy? The cartoon people told me to ask you because they knew you'd know the answer."

Me: "If you ever wake me up to ask me something about cartoon people again, please lie and tell me something truly terrible has happened, like your arm has fallen off or your face is being eaten off by weevils!"

I woke up the next morning completely convinced that there was no possible way I could make it through the day. I was so totally exhausted, in every way spent—emotionally, spiritually, physically. And I had a terrible headache. One so bad that I was sure if I looked in the mirror, I would find my eyeballs had moved to the sides of my head like a catfish and my forehead had bulged out so far it would rest against the windshield while I was driving. And that can't be safe!

It was a big day, a busy day full of travel and doctor's exams and visits with therapists. And when it was time for the day to begin, to hop out of bed and get going, I didn't want to. Something managed to pry me out of that warm cocoon, though. Something short, blond and preschoolish, eager for a toaster waffle. Her voice sounded like many, many trumpets, so loud that my brain shook inside my skull like a marble when she spoke.

This grueling lifestyle was like the American Fitness evaluations I had in grade school. Mind you, I'm not even a remotely healthy person, unless you count those eleven gummy vitamins of Lily's I had eaten back in our rehab days. One of the school fitness tests was to run a mile, and of course they used a stopwatch to keep time, but an oven timer would have worked just as well at my pace. Or a sundial, for that matter.

We needed to run six laps around the football field. When my best friend and I got halfway done, we would be 99 percent sure we were dying and fake simultaneous asthma attacks. (We were eleven, okay?)

I always ended up finishing those races. Really, really close to last place sometimes. Walking a bit, clutching my side toward the end and gulping for air most unattractively, but I finished. I made it through the difficult day of doctoring and travel, too, my endurance thin, stretched and frayed, sure to break. Paul's words resonated like never before, "Forgetting what is behind . . . I press on toward the goal" (Philippians 3:13–14). Maybe it's really true that at the end of our strength, Christ's own power in us is more obvious.

Even so, I had things to ask God. "Doesn't it say somewhere in Your Book that You grant rest to those You love? Over and over again, You promised rest if we would come to You. Why doesn't it come?" I questioned as I put the last dish in the dishwasher, shoved some towels in the mountain of dirty laundry and checked to see that all the doors were secure.

When finally the last house light was turned off, I stumbled through the dark like a half-squished spider, crumbly but still going. The kind you don't know exactly what to do with—do you mercifully step on it and put it out of its misery? Or just let it keep on going because it can?

What started as a gentle thunderstorm outside became furiously intense as I finally crawled into bed. And so I crossed the house again to carry Lily over to our room. I wanted to avoid a lot of drama if she woke up frightened. So it was the three of us plus a crotchety cat in an overstuffed room. Allen was in his hospital bed that we had tried to disguise with homey bedding and pillows. Lily and I were in a small bed pushed up against the wall. We were dwarfed by all the clumsy, bulky medical equipment around us: a standing frame, a lift, a finally vacant wheelchair charging by the wall for the night.

I closed my eyes, not that it made any difference. It was pitch-black either way, except for the lightning that lit up the room like a strobe light every few seconds. Lightning struck hard and fast, seemingly in our very backyard, so that there was no delay between the light and the booming thunder. The crash brought me straight up in bed, but thankfully Allen and Lily slept through it.

I prayed in my mind, with no thought or real faith, *Please, God, would You just put Your hand over our house so I can sleep in Your peace?*

The exact moment I thought those words, the rainstorm abruptly stopped just over the top of us. It didn't ease off or gently slow to a stop. The end was sudden and shocking. I could hear rain falling in a circle all around us, but no longer falling on our rooftop. And then I saw lightning and counted to nine before hearing a soft rumble in the distance. I was so shocked that God had actually heard my little throwaway prayer, one I hadn't really given any serious thought to.

The next morning, I called home to tell my parents what had happened. While on the phone with them my sister beeped in, so I talked to her a minute and told her the whole story, too. When I did, she got all blubbery and mushy, which isn't that weird for her. She is so sentimental and tenderhearted, she would probably get emotional reading the ingredients on a potato chip bag.

"You're kidding me!" she said.

"Why would I kid about that?" I asked.

She continued, "A song just came on the radio, and I felt as if I had to call you with the lyrics."

"What on earth was it?" I asked her.

She recited, "Sometimes He calms the storm and other times He calms His child . . ."

8

A DOTING DAD

the weather turned cold. Lights and holly began creeping up in all the usual places. Smiles began emerging more easily from just about everyone just about everywhere, except in store parking lots. A man in my blind spot cut me off in traffic, but I tried to smile in spite of it—even though he honked brazenly and waved oddly, as if to say, "You're number one."

Every year for Christmas, we would travel up north to celebrate with Allen's family and mine. We wouldn't make it this year. We didn't know when or if we would ever make it. It was an eight-hour drive and just not possible yet. While I was driving across town, the song "I'll Be Home for Christmas" came on the radio. I thought about getting weepy, but chose instead to turn it off. I was amazed at how well that worked!

But later that night, I prayed, "God, it's coming on Christmas, and everywhere people are merry. At a time when hearts are supposed to feel full, mine doesn't feel like a solid thing at all. More like something you scoop out of a bowl with chips. Is there some kind of time limit for socially acceptable miserableness? I feel like a big whiner, what with the way I come begging to You day in and day out. I want so badly for You to deliver my family. It isn't that my prolific whining brings me comfort, but coming to You is all I know how to do. Never a minute passes by that we don't love and want You. I'm sure glad You're up there."

A dozen people must have asked if Allen needed help Christmas shopping, and I wanted to say something funny like "Where have you been the past thirteen years of our marriage?" But instead, I replied something like "Please, no, I beg of you," and I meant it. I so badly wanted Christmas Day to come and go without any fuss.

Normally, I love Christmas and our home belches up colorful lights everywhere, as if it overdosed on Froot Loops. I've even gone so far and been so lame as to color-coordinate the wrappings under the tree.

This year was different. I was mostly saddened by the news that my parents and my sister wouldn't make it down our way due to a snowstorm that had settled across the Midwest. My two brothers and their families braved the dangerous drifts to come and be with us, and we loved every minute with them! Allen's family came, too. It meant so much to have them all close.

Not long after everyone had gone, when the roads were dry and schedules cleared, my parents did pack up to visit us. I was elated, deliriously awaiting their arrival. Finally, the morning came. Giddy with excitement, we discussed pressing matters as I got Allen in and out of the shower and cut his whiskers.

"I think a funny parody CD would be the Benedictine Munch-kins," I suggested.

"Munchkins? Now there's a large people group you don't want to offend," Allen said.

"Not *very* large," I smirked.

"Do my socks match?" he interrogated me as I got him loaded up in the chair. He knew he needed to ask. Let's just say that often, my standards weren't quite as high as his when it came to the details.

We experimented by singing as loudly and off-tune as we could in an effort to chase the always annoyed cat out of the room of her own volition. It totally worked!

When Allen was all put together and matching, I gussied up the house, vacuumed around a pair of pants that had been lying on the floor for a week and fixed a pot of soup and some hot bread. I checked the clock every few minutes, wondering about Mom and Dad's progress on the road.

Thoughts of them made me terribly homesick for my small hometown. *Am I ever going to get up there again?* I wondered as I looked out the window eagerly for a midsized silver car.

I was born the youngest of four to a gentle, humble Swedish preacher who spent most of his life giving to a tiny farm town in Iowa. It was a charming place, full of sweet smells in summer and blankets of thick snow in winter. The town had only a post office, a bank, a tavern and a church, *our* church—a big, beautiful church with complicated stained-glass windows and ceilings as tall as the Sistine Chapel.

Most Sundays, my beloved dad preached that Jesus was return-ing, a message I took so much to heart that I would often lie in our grassy backyard and stare up at the sky, waiting for the action to begin at any moment.

Mom was a dreamboat—beautiful, smart, funny, strict, yet never unreasonable. She kept everything humming and never raised her voice. If the Bible didn't say otherwise, I would be completely convinced that she has never made a mistake to this day.

Growing up, our house was filled with music and laughter. Everyone played an instrument, and my sister and brothers could sing like heaven's angels. We chased fireflies on summer nights after church, sledded down huge snow mountains, played football with our slobbery dog and held our breath when we walked near the liquor aisle of the grocery store. Somehow, without taking it for granted, I knew I had the best parents and family life in the world.

In a moment of nostalgia, I went to the computer and Google-earthed little Liscomb, Iowa. The satellite images were amazing. I could see the houses, the grass, the trees, the streets I had zipped around on, riding my small blue bike with a banana seat. That virtual visit made me really, really depressed. I closed the laptop and went back to work.

The kitchen smelled of coffee and yeast rolls, which transported me back to childhood visits to Grandma Peterson's house where we all gathered around a huge dining table for hours. She had taught us all a Swedish prayer we would say together before digging into gastronomic wonders galore. The warmth of her kitchen made things feel cozy.

I came back to the real world and began putting away clothes balls—Lily had just learned to "fold" laundry. She was proud of her accomplishment.

"When I was a baby, did you even know I was going to be this great?" she asked.

"I had *no idea*." I smiled.

The rubber alligator in her tight, sweaty hand jerked back into action to pursue the mistreated princess doll in her other hand.

"I'm going to eat you up, my healthy little snack," the green monster growled in a sweet, husky voice.

As the princess met her unexpected demise, I scrubbed the toilet, then stood back and cocked my head, wondering why the strangely clean white bowl looked so odd to me. I guess it had been a while.

The glass on our front storm door had at least a dozen nose prints from Lily pressing her face against it, the way all kids do. After what seemed like a long wait, she finally squealed, "They're here!"

She and I raced down the ramp onto the cold driveway with no thought of putting on shoes. My parents' backs and legs were sore and stiff from such a long ride, so they were moving more slowly. Seeing Dad coming toward me reminded me of a Sunday night at church when I was eight years old. I had wanted to be baptized but was so shy and afraid, I couldn't bring myself to walk down that long aisle. Dad wasn't disappointed in me or pushy. He had said reassuringly, "Sis, if you start down the aisle, I'll meet you halfway." And he did. I ran into his arms now, just as I had then.

There were shrieks, laughs and smiles, and I squeezed my parents so tightly that they must have feared bodily damage! We began carrying in armfuls of things. They planned to stay two or three weeks! We couldn't decide what to do first. We would put a few things in place, then visit a bit, then eat a little something. Lily recited for us the books of the Old Testament. She'd been practicing for weeks. "Chewbacca" and "Levitation" made the list.

"Now wouldn't that spice up Sunday school?" I commented. We were all laughing and feeling good. It was like someone threw the sun on in a house that had been sort of dim.

If God was anything like my earthly father, I knew He must be completely kindly. Dad was such a kindhearted person that if the gleams of loving wonderfulness shooting out of his eyes were actual laser beams, he could use them to chisel ice sculptures for civic events and make tons of money, which he would then in turn give to the poor, only furthering his wonderfulness.

It became a challenge to try to catch Dad doing anything other than reading his Bible, journaling in his prayer notebook, watching or listening to preaching or praise music or encouraging someone through an e-mail or phone call. He and Mom were such a help to us in every way, but somehow we all knew that the spiritual comfort they brought was the real reason they were here.

One morning, the whole house smelled like fresh coffee. The late morning sun was pouring in. Dad sat, cup in hand, as Mom cleared away the dishes. Allen and I had missed breakfast, as we did most mornings. It took longer than you might think to look as disheveled as we did.

Dad's heart was totally open to God, and his faith was truly like that of a child, innocent and inspiring. He had some great stories to tell.

"We're going to keep praying, Sis, for two miracles: Allen and me. God will come through!" he urged. Then, he told us the story of his friend Harold who had been healed of multiple sclerosis.

At 33, Harold Selby, a beloved high school teacher, had been diagnosed by the Mayo Clinic with a severe form of multiple sclerosis. It was considered untreatable and irreversible. His story is told in Kathryn Kuhlman's book *God Can Do It Again* (Bridge-Logos, 1993), but Dad knew him firsthand.

Over the months following his diagnosis, Harold's condition quickly deteriorated. He was from a more traditional denomination and had never heard of anyone being healed by Jesus in modern times. One day, a man gave him a book about modern-day miracles. Harold didn't know what to make of the strange reports that people were being healed, but after months of diligent searching and physical decline, Harold and Arlene, his wife, knew they had to go to a healing service in Pennsylvania.

Harold sold encyclopedias to raise the money needed for their trip. The journey was a difficult one, but they made it to the meeting. At one point, Arlene reached down and took tight hold of Harold's hand. A small African American woman reached out to hold his other hand, but he hesitated, offering her only the last two fingers of his left hand. She held onto them tightly.

A wave of guilt fell over him. "Forgive me, Lord," he said, "I should have offered her my whole hand." As he prayed this, what felt like electricity went through his body, and he was perfectly, instantly healed!

He returned home, able to return to the work he had loved— teaching school. He was even promoted to principal, and he told everyone what Jesus had done for him.

"Yes," I nodded. I remembered the Selbys. My childhood friend had taken piano lessons from Arlene, and even at that time they were still giving glory to God for Harold's healing.

Dad told another story of a friend, Bill, whom he had prayed with in the hospital. Bill, the town postmaster, had become blind in one eye over the course of his cancer treatments. Bill was usually warm and cheery, but this day, he felt discouraged. He was no longer able to read. When Dad prayed with him, Bill's blind eye was opened! Bill's unbelieving roommate then asked for prayer. He was also dying of cancer and was in the final stages. On a later hospital visit, Dad learned that Bill's roommate had soon afterward been discharged, his cancer gone!

"God is still God," Dad encouraged. "Still full of compassion."

Dad's unshakeable trust in God resonated even more loudly than the incredible stories of faith and victory he shared. He had recently been diagnosed with Parkinson's disease, and each day it continued to be a nuisance. The coffee cup in his right hand shook a bit as he took it to his mouth because of a pesky tremor, an unwelcome reminder of the disease's assault on his body. But his confidence in God only grew!

Dad would often spend an entire day reading the Bible. He read through the whole thing in just weeks with the efficiency of a machine. His trust in God reminded me of the way Jesus trusted His heavenly Father. Jesus surrendered completely to His Father's will, allowing Himself to suffer and be murdered. Jesus did remarkable things on earth, but in this last act of ultimate submission, He would trust the Spirit of God to raise Him from the dead—never worrying about whether or not His Dad would leave Him in the grave. Of course not! Jesus didn't have a hint of doubt about the Father's goodness or love for Him!

My dad did not suppose to know the future, but he had nothing but complete certainty in his spirit about how God felt toward him, and he knew who God was. God was good to him 100 percent of the time, and Dad's disposition was therefore immovable. I so admired his steely resolve, even as his condition seemingly worsened.

I was beginning to wonder if the Kingdom of God belonged to the presumptuous—those who didn't waffle and wonder about whether God's love and promises were meant for them. They just assumed it was so and grabbed on tenaciously. Like blind Bartimaeus, who just kept on shouting his head off until Jesus came his way (see Mark 10:46–52).

With Mom and Dad around, I had a little more freedom to come and go, so on an unseasonably warm day, I took Lily to a nearby playground. Many families were there. While she played, I rehearsed some memory verses from Matthew chapter 7: "Ask and it will be given to you; seek and you will find; knock and the door will be opened to you," I began (verse 7), noticing a very gruff-looking young father across the way. *Speaking of doors, I thought, we should lock ours more often.*

"For everyone who asks receives; he who seeks finds; and to him who knocks, the door will be opened," I continued (verse 8). The twentysomething dad had an unsightly cigarette dangling from his mouth, and tattoos covered his body. He frequently cursed as he talked to the woman sitting next to him.

"Which of you, if his son asks for bread, will give him a stone? Or if he asks for a fish, will give him a snake?" (verses 9–10). I suspiciously kept my gaze on the shady young man. All at once, his toddler shot into his open arms, squealing.

"If you, then, though you are evil, know how to give good gifts to your children, how much more will your Father in heaven give good gifts to those who ask him!" I quoted in my mind (verse 11). Just at that moment, the young man lovingly tossed his baby girl high into the air. A grin as wide as bananas spread across her face, her eyes squinting with delight. Then he smothered her with kisses, and she giggled as he tickled her belly with his whiskers. I was all choked up as I watched the verses play out before me.

I had the best, most loving dad the world could possibly cough up. If anyone could point me to the goodness and kindness of God, it would be him. "So in everything, do to others what you would have them do to you, for this sums up the Law and the Prophets," I rehearsed (verse 12), finishing out the passage. That last verse stuck me good. *When I doubt God's goodness toward me, I'm sort of accusing Him of being a lawbreaker.* I winced inwardly.

I thought about the first sin, the *biggie* sin in the Garden of Eden as Eve mulled over the serpent's allegations. In effect, the serpent told her, "God is holding out on you. He doesn't want you to have as much as He does. He can't be trusted. He doesn't love you that much."

Of course, had it been me in the garden, I'd have gumbled it up just because the temptation involved food. I love food.

The devil still plants those doubts today, I mused. Later that night, as Dad sat in a recliner and listened to gospel music on TV, I sat at his feet, my head resting on his knee. (I wished the moment could last a thousand years.) Dad's gentle hand stroked my head while I tried to wrap my brain around the Father-love God feels toward us. It seemed way too good to be true.

9

THE WHISPERS OF GOD

the books I had illustrated were published. I opened the package excitedly when it arrived, anxious to see them for the first time. It was a thrill—yet it didn't change anything. At the end of the day, Allen still wanted his nose cleaned out and Lily was clamoring for a sandwich. To be honest, I was surprised that it had been such a futile chase, that whole "dreams and aspirations" thing about my career. Like the time I panted and puffed and wheezed on a high-tech elliptical machine to burn about fourteen calories. Careers and elliptical machines had both sunk way lower on my list of priorities these days.

It was wonderful to have my parents still with us, and they were so helpful with our almost all-consuming needs. Allen was making good use of his arm strength, and he made a trip or two in to the Campus Ministry site at Rolla, where he worked for a few hours each week to offer whatever help and advice he could. But he just wasn't able to return to business as usual or keep the kind of hours he would have liked.

A lack of muscle function wasn't the only thing working against him. He was in almost constant, unexplainable neurological pain—burning, stinging, excruciating pain. And since his body was no longer able to regulate temperature, he constantly needed more clothes on, or less, to stay comfortable. And menthol for his sore shoulders. And a hankie. And a drink of water. And his laptop plugged in. I wasn't always as patient as I should have been. It was like my chair was spring-loaded with an ejector switch that sprang whenever I went to sit down.

The daily grind was relentless. Allen was usually laid-back, but sometimes he became moody when pain or frustration got the better of him. And I would tire of things revolving around what other people needed. Sometimes I would lose my cool. The words of 1 Corinthians 13 would torment me, that things only count if they are done lovingly. Occasionally I did a good job of holding things together, even when I felt deep down that I was justified in my irritation. Other times I blew it.

"We don't really talk anymore, we just kind of communicate in to-do lists," I chided Allen.

Lily was catching on, too. One morning while I got dressed, she crept up beside me and reported, "I just thought you should know that the closet light is on and the toilet bowl is dirty."

"Thanks, Allen," I muttered back under my breath, amused by her likeness to her daddy.

Lily was also becoming a big help around the house, and Allen often had small jobs for her to do. She once whispered in my ear sincerely, "Is Daddy faking it just to get us to serve him?"

Her question made me laugh out loud. "Boy, is he in trouble if he is!" I quipped back with a smile.

The upside to all the menial tasks was that the things I used to waste a lot of time on melted away painlessly, without a lot of grunt work and discipline on my part. I wouldn't have considered myself a television junkie or someone overly engrossed in computers, but now I didn't have time for either. I was surprised by the swell of relief I felt at not having to keep up with celebrity cosmetic surgery disasters or who looked bloated at the Oscars. Even though I had always considered my media standards pretty stringent, I came to realize that I really had been taking in a lot of junk. Malachi 3:18 came to mind, that God looks for a distinction between the evil and the righteous. Even though this new way of thinking came on rather accidentally, I didn't want to go back.

I had always been troubled by Jesus saying that His sheep would hear His voice. *Why can't I hear it?* I had wondered. But since the world wasn't constantly hollering in my ear anymore, I really could hear Him better. Countless times in the past, I had felt an urge to go visit someone who was sick, or pray with someone I had only just met or reach out to someone holding a Will Work for Food sign. But I had often reasoned myself out of it, unconvinced it was actually God's voice at work in me.

"I think that quiet voice urging me along is the Holy Spirit," I confessed to Allen. "He's been there all the time, I guess, but I think I've been grieving Him because I don't always obey. Starting today, I'm going to do whatever I feel He is asking me to do, the first time He asks me to do it," I determined.

Allen looked skeptical, but grinned in a sweet way, as if to say, "That's awesome, go for it—this probably won't work."

I started out with great fervor. I drove to a nearby nursing facility, sat down at the piano in their dining room and praised

God as they ate. People looked confused, but no one questioned whether or not I should be there. Success! I felt a thrilling surge, eager for my next assignment.

My parents were with Allen, so I headed over to pray for a kind, elderly man whom I often transported around town. He was hunchbacked and had some other problems, and he lived in a tiny shed in someone's backyard. It made me sad, although he was doing well and was very independent—paying his bills, getting where he needed to go. He had about three shirts and three pairs of pants. They were all the same, and often I would see them hanging on a clothesline outside his shack.

I drove him to the eye doctor for a new pair of spectacles to replace his broken ones, and then felt I should pray for his healing. I asked if I could pray with him, and he didn't really understand. I put my hand on his back and started in, but he thought I was hugging him and he reached out to hug me back. He was so happy to be hugged! I don't know if he had ever been hugged.

I continued my prayer, but he thought we were just conversing. "Pretty day today, isn't it?" he beamed midstream.

That went a little weirdly, I thought as I eventually crawled back into my car. But I still wasn't derailed. I was happy and proud that I was finally obeying the Spirit of God inside me.

My last stop was the pharmacy we used in a supersized shopping center. At once, my eyes fell on a lady who had a terrible problem with her leg and foot. Instead of facing forward, her foot faced to the side. She dragged it behind her when she walked.

"Noooo, God!" I begged. Without conscious awareness, I had turned my shopping cart in the opposite direction like Jonah, God's oh-so-human prophet. After a moment, cooler heads prevailed. Surely this wasn't God's voice I was hearing.

"God, I'm going to the vitamin aisle. This place is huge. If she's in the vitamin aisle—if she's in front of the children's vitamins in the vitamin aisle," I negotiated, "I'll know that was really Your voice telling me to pray for her. If not, I'll know it was just my overactive guilt complex at work."

I approached the aisle gravely. To my consternation, there she was, right in front of the children's vitamins. I stalked her for six aisles, all the way to the shampoo. And then I heard myself saying in the smallest voice, "Could I pray with you?"

Silence.

"I think God wants me to pray a blessing on you," I awkwardly repeated, barely audible.

Silence. Annoyance. Then softer resistance.

"I never let people do that," she crabbed, "but go ahead."

And I continued with the shortest, dumbest prayer ever muttered, ever. It was about ten seconds long. Ten *long* seconds long. I opened my tightly squinted eyes—no change. And of course, for an hour I kept running into her again and again all through the store.

"God, she can't even go to the store in peace! I've ruined her day and made her feel like a spectacle! Please don't let her turn away from You on account of me! Please heal her and show Your kindness to her even though my prayer was bad!"

She and I both sloughed through the parking lot to our cars at about the same time, and all my excitement and resolve waved good-bye like a disingenuous stewardess who thoughtlessly pats you on the back as you exit the plane.

That could have gone better, I thought with a healthy dose of disillusionment. I doubted whether or not I really could discern God's voice in me. It seemed that just as often, the quiet voice in my head spoke something to me like *"Chocolate!"*

Almost every night that my parents were with us, we prayed together. Praying with a man of faith like my dad was extraordinary. One night, Dad placed his hands on Allen's shoulders and prayed. I was sitting on the floor at Allen's feet, looking up. Dad's face had a particular glow. The words of Psalm 34:5 came to my mind, that those who look to the Lord have radiant faces never darkened with shame . . .

Sometimes when we prayed, Dad's hand would grow hot in mine, and I would remember James 5:16 (KJV)—"The effectual fervent prayer of a righteous man availeth much." I had looked *fervent* up in a dictionary once and was surprised to see "extremely hot and glowing" listed as a definition. Dad's faith and prayers were powerful.

Other times it was if Dad could feel the Lord's touch in an almost tangible way. But still, his tremors were as bothersome as ever, and Allen still wasn't able to feel anything or do the Macarena.

The night before my parents left, Allen and I quarreled. I was mustering every shred of splintered faith I could find in me to keep hoping that God would intervene and heal these two guys I loved so much. But we were both so discouraged. And while Allen genuinely appreciated the prayers, he wasn't convinced that God still moves in those ways today.

"I think it wouldn't be bad for us just to accept things and move on," he told me soberly.

"I'm willing to give up anything God asks of me, but I don't want to surrender anything the devil is trying to steal," I replied cautiously. I was coming to believe that Satan was the thief coming to steal and destroy. That God intended His church to function as He left it, which at least offered the hope that with faith in prayer, Allen might recover. "Surely God would have said *something* to that effect before He left if He meant it to be different?" I argued.

I had recently read Mark 16:17–20, Jesus' last words before zooping back up into heaven. My eyes bulged when I saw it. I don't think I had ever realized it was part of the Great Commission:

> And these signs will accompany those who believe: In my name they will drive out demons; they will speak in new tongues; they will pick up snakes with their hands; and when they drink deadly poison, it will not hurt them at all; they will place their hands on sick people, and they will get well.
>
> After the Lord Jesus had spoken to them, he was taken up into heaven and he sat at the right hand of God. Then the disciples went out and preached everywhere, and the Lord worked with them and confirmed his word by the signs that accompanied it.

"It's the *Great Commission*—we talk about that all the time. If we readily embrace that Jesus' marching commands apply to us, couldn't we expect Him to be just as present a help in fulfilling them?" I earnestly questioned Allen.

"Your dad is the most godly man I know. If God hasn't healed him, what hope do any of us have?" Allen rationalized. He brought up other examples, too, of men and women of God, including his dad, who had not been healed after years of prayer.

I didn't know what to say. The only thing I knew for sure was that I wasn't right about stuff all of the time.

After I got Allen in bed, I got on my knees. I pleaded with God to please heal my dad so that Allen's faith might be encouraged. I passionately uttered these exact bossy words: "God, I need Your eyes on me right now. I need Your ears listening to my prayer!"

At that moment, I noticed the Bible beside my knees was opened to 1 Peter 3:12: "For the eyes of the Lord are on the righteous and his ears are attentive to their prayer." I was beginning to realize that when the book of Hebrews describes God's Word as alive and active, that's a literal thing. And even though it sounds cliché, yes, God really does speak to us through His Word.

God hears us when we pray! It was an overwhelming realization for me. Can you even believe that? The one who made Saturn and the Northern Lights, and who thought up things like sea horses and cattails and ears of corn, knew exactly where to find me, sore knees boring into my cold, hard bedroom floor in the dark. He could list all thirteen snacks I had eaten that day and tell in perfect verbatim my most secret thoughts. And somewhere in heaven, really close to God, an angel sits, pen in hand—or laser pen or really shiny marker, whatever they use to write stuff in heaven. Malachi 3:16 says that good things about God's people are recorded in a *Book of Remembrance*. Nothing is missed or forgotten.

Even though I was so totally disappointed that my prayers weren't getting the answers I was hoping for, it was somehow enough that night to know that they were heard and that what I did was remembered.

My parents loaded up their car and left the next day. Dad was still shuffling, coping with painful joints and trembling hands. I was so sad to see their silver car getting smaller and smaller as they drove away. They called several times en route to check on me, and I was already lonely for them.

Luckily, Lily offered comic relief. She had hidden a bunch of their stuff in her closet, figuring they would need to turn around and come back for it.

10

FRIED CHICKEN
AND PRIORITIES

I stepped into our church's fellowship hall, a big, mostly empty gray gym with folding tables set up haphazardly. At the front was a makeshift stage of carpeted wooden squares pushed together. Its stark, unfinished plainness gave it charm.

The preacher's wife, Jana, was at a table full of college-aged girls. She was cracking jokes in her usual spunky way. I sat down at their table, plate of fried chicken in hand. Anytime we have a fellowship dinner, there is fried chicken. I'm not really sure if it's because people like the fried chicken that much, or if it's just part of the program, like Sunday bulletins, taking up an offering and "Let's have fried chicken."

"Where's Big Al?" Jana asked.

"He wanted to be alone for a minute. He's praying, I think," I explained. It sounded weird to me as I heard myself saying it. But Jana wasn't put off; she continued on making everyone laugh and feel good.

Then, I could not believe my eyes—Allen came walking in! People began screaming and falling to their knees to thank and praise God!

Allen came over to where I was. "God spoke to me audibly!" he said. He explained that God had told him seven things, and he shared one with me, something to do with gentleness. We were hugging and crying and thanking God.

And then I woke up. It had been a dream. I could not believe it was a dream; it seemed so incredibly real! In fact, I wondered if it was something more. A ninety-year-old saint at church had looked me squarely in the eye at least three times and said convincingly, soberly, "God is going to call him out of that chair."

Meanwhile, just now someone else was calling *me* out of bed. The long nights and stress were taking their toll. My hair was getting thin and scraggly (think adolescent boy's first mustache). *Good grief*, I contemplated as I caught sight of myself in the mirror, *my newly wrinkled face looks like a piece of chewed gum.* A few years ago, the scene would have sent me reeling, but now it was the least of my problems. Unsettling, but not terribly upsetting.

I drove Lily to school, then I put Allen together. As on a lot of mornings (summer, spring or fall), I started the day by playing a really annoying, four-hand piano rendition of "Sleigh Ride" on my iPod for laughs. I added my own dance moves, which Allen endured good-naturedly. Then he watched with dismay as I untangled a long hair from the toothpaste lid before loading up his brush.

Fried Chicken and Priorities

"Way to sell the product," he moaned dryly. People always missed how funny he was because of his poker face.

Later in the afternoon, neighborhood kids came over to play, just as they always had before the accident. They were curious about most everything, including the weird bag on Allen's leg, which had yellow liquid inside.

"That's my oil bag," Allen teasingly lied.

They seemed satisfied. Their curiosity and openness actually made things less awkward.

I was cleaning out the medicine cupboard that was brimming over. I found a bunch of respiratory masks, the kind you wear in an all-out black plague epidemic or a bad case of halitosis. Since the plague wasn't on my itinerary for the week, I offered the masks to the kids to play with.

I always liked when kids came over to play, and I greatly amused myself by seeing what kind of dumb stuff I could get them to do. I suggested they wear the masks on their heads as hats, and we played a game of Rabbi, May I, the game more commonly known as Mother, May I—this time with the addition of little masks worn on top of the head.

Something in the game was a metaphor for our life, which involved a lot of asking things of God (begging, actually) and hoping He would move us forward. It seemed sometimes God agreed, letting us proceed slowly, inch by inch. Sometimes He said no. And sometimes we found ourselves set back so far on our rumps that it seemed we'd been sent rocketing backward from a human cannon.

The kids gathered around our small kitchen table for Cheez Doodles. More doodles landed on the floor than in their mouths. Our hissy cat, Lola, lurked around suspiciously, giving everyone the stink eye. Then she batted CJ, the three-year-old neighbor boy, on the forehead with her paw.

97

NORTHFIELD PUBLIC LIBRARY
210 Washington Street
Northfield, MN 55057

Lola was rescued from an animal shelter, but with a preschooler around the house, I'm not sure we were doing Lola the cat any favors. Most days she had that look in her eye, as if she were reminiscing with great fondness about the good old days in her two-by-two-foot cell. That cat did *not* like kids.

CJ didn't seem to notice. "She gave me a high five! Right here on the head!" he jubilantly announced.

"You're a juice-box-is-half-full kind of kid." I smirked.

I wish I had that kind of optimism, like that of the apostles, who praised God that they could share in the suffering of Christ. Or like Joseph, who held on for years to the dreams of his youth through betrayal, slavery and imprisonment. I think at some point I would have given up my dreams and thought, *Maybe I just ate some bad cheese before bed.*

After a snack, the kids got busy decorating the basement in the exact likeness of a war-torn amusement park that had been in the path of a merciless cyclone. And I began the grim job of resetting all the digital clocks that had goobered up in a recent power surge.

As I started punching in numbers on the microwave, it asked me the date.

"Why does a microwave need to know the date?" I grumped. "It pretty much just needs to know how to cook a bag of popcorn."

The cheesy philosophical side of me made some deep connection, though. I thought, *Hey, maybe it's that way for God. We bombard Him with questions He doesn't really think we need to know the answers to. He just wants us to trust Him.*

I found myself praying, "God, how much peace do I miss out on because I worry about things You don't care about—ambitions, back fat, heap-piles of laundry, dishes undone and the premature signs of aging? Thanks for such a good life. You've been

NORTHFIELD PUBLIC LIBRARY
210 Washington Street
Northfield, MN 55057

amazing to me, and I'm sorry for every moment that I've failed to acknowledge You."

At times, I couldn't help but feel like a phony when I tried to be upbeat. But sometimes I really, truly felt grateful way down deep, in spite of our troubles—even though I know it must sound impossible.

Amazingly, I made dinner. I wasn't receiving the praise I thought I deserved, though, so I did that thing women do so proficiently. I fished for compliments and then got really mad when they didn't materialize. How do we as a people group perfect this art with no formal training whatsoever, only instinct to guide us?

"This chicken is pretty good," I baited.

Every time I shoveled a fork into Allen's mouth, my own mouth opened, just as it did when Lily was a baby and I held a spoon of green goo to her lips. Allen made the same face, openly mocking me, and we laughed. For my own amusement, I staved off boredom by getting creative with my delivery techniques, taking a buttered roll to his lips one way, and then another.

I baited my hook a second time: "I like this chicken recipe. It's good, don't you think?"

As it turned out, Allen didn't really like the chicken much, and he said so.

I said some stuff after that. Estrogeny fuming, mostly. One of the most difficult challenges in our situation is that even when I am super mad at Allen, I can't storm off and cool down, as one might normally do. I just have to stay right there and keep on doing a bunch of chores for him. That's hard!

Evening settled in. Lily was asleep. Allen was in bed without the TV remote, which brought me a ghoulish hilarity because a really, really goofy show was on a Christian network. He really *was* becoming adept at long-suffering.

I sat down on the couch and assessed the damages—our once tidy house was now ignored and almost always looked disheveled. A mountain of clothes sat beside me, waiting to be folded. That was all the incentive I needed to open my Bible, now so worn that the covers and pages curled backward like calligraphy letters. I read John 15:7 "If you remain in me and my words remain in you, ask whatever you wish, and it will be given you."

That was a pretty good promise. It struck me that I should be memorizing Scripture more. *I have a bad brain*, I waffled. Flashback to finding our house phone under the bathroom sink. And my purse in the dryer. And two boxes of Velcro in the refrigerator. And I've probably already mentioned that elsewhere, but I already forgot because my brain is that bad. Mostly, to find Scriptures I had always relied on my scribbled-up Bible, concordances. High-speed Internet to help me find the exact verses I needed. "You'll have to help me, Lord," I determined.

I find it interesting that God often asks us to do the things we feel least equipped for. *What next?* I wondered, trying to imagine what weakness in me God might want to use. Cooking? Knitting? Bad Frisbee throwing?

This verse, this plan of God is masterful, I thought. *How disastrous would it be if everyone got whatever they asked God for? We'd become proud, or become hotshots or ask for stuff that is really dumb,* I considered. Then I thought about how, when we invest ourselves in God's Word, when it becomes a part of us, our identity, we begin to seek and pray for His will to be done. Those are prayers He's *eager* to answer! And crowds are drawn to Him as they begin to see miraculous answers to the prayers of His people.

John 1:1 refers to Jesus as the *Word*. I never totally got that. But I was coming to think it meant God could not be separated from His Word, spoken or written. And when you take the Word into your heart, it's like taking the Spirit of God inside you. The One who spoke the universe into existence is available to anyone willing to take Scripture to heart. I already knew much of the Sermon on the Mount, so I decided that maybe trying to memorize the book of Matthew would be a good place to start.

I knew I needed more of the Word in me and more time to get it there, as well as more time to do everything else required of me in our current situation. I explained to Wendy Lynn, my art agent, that I needed to take a leave of absence from my illustration work until "who knows when." I had so little free time that it just seemed more important to spend it chasing God and standing in the gap for my gimpy family. I was thankful that Wendy was so gracious and cool about it all. In fact, she probably would have offered to run guns across the border if she thought it would help, even though she probably should have dropped me like a hot potato.

Allen and I had continued to work in small snatches when we could, but for the most part the accident had yanked both of us out of the work force. It was humbling and embarrassing to rely on disability income to make ends meet, but it was necessary for now. Tragedy had shifted my priorities. God and family were all that really mattered.

II

CLIMBS AND PLUNGES

It was always a temptation to wallow in our disappointments, and people expected us to wallow. Everyone was so tenderhearted toward us. Whenever I attended a Bible study or visited with a longtime friend, they would look somber, eyes fixed, eyebrows raised. "How are you, *really*?" they would ask, their voice lower, softer.

I never knew what would come tumbling out of my mouth— some days determined optimism! "Quite well, actually," I'd report with confidence. Other days, I'd spin through a litany of complaints that probably made them very sorry they had asked.

And it was almost comical to see a yard full of laughing, jovial college students who were tossing a football around and having fun—until suddenly they'd spot our enormous handicap van pulling into the parking lot. Their faces would fall and look sad, as if they felt bad to be playing, laughing and having fun when Allen couldn't do the same. Handicap vans just make people sad, so we nicknamed the van the "Bummermobile."

Allen stayed wildly positive almost always, and I found comfort by reading the testimonies of those who had been healed. *I want to immerse myself in stories that have the kind of outcome I'm hoping for,* I told myself.

One testimony was about a lovely lady, Marlene Klepees, whom I read about in Pat Robertson's *Miracles Can Be Yours Today* (Integrity, 2006). Marlene had been born with a case of debilitating cerebral palsy. In addition to being stricken herself with spastic quadriplegia, she had lost her parents. They died in a motorcycle accident when she was a toddler, and she was raised by grandparents and in foster homes. Her story was moving and surprising, and I noticed that she lived only an hour and a half away from us.

I should call her! I thought. I'm not sure where that idea came from, since I probably could live three weeks straight off of nothing but my meaty hatred of talking on the phone. I tried for days to work up the courage to call, but I kept chickening out. On a beautiful spring morning, cell phone in pocket, I walked around the house and admired the new greenness. I had loaded Marlene's number into my phone on one of my many other dialing attempts, and now I stared at it several times on my phone screen, as if I might push the green Talk button, but I didn't.

Finally, I sat down on our retaining wall and made myself push the button, nervously waiting for a voice on the other end. Marlene answered, and we fell easily into conversation. I lost all track of time. No one would have ever known by hearing Marlene's voice that people used to have difficulty understanding her when she spoke. She was such a kindly person, wise like a well-spoken Bible college professor, and so untouched by worldliness. I listened with delight to her story.

She was born prematurely, weighing only two pounds. Her cerebral palsy had become so severe in her youth that she couldn't even hold her head erect or swallow properly. Her mind was sharp and alert, but she couldn't easily communicate and struggled to do anything for herself. Her aging grandparents were becoming unable to care for her, and she was terrified of going to a nursing home.

She found herself at the Mayo Clinic in Minnesota. As a teenager, she had heard of Jesus' healing power, and she put her hope in Him. As a young adult, her situation was still as dire as ever. In frustration, she called out to God angrily. Moved by His great compassion, God gave her a vision of a church where people were praying for her, and of her being healed. And then she saw herself riding a bicycle in the countryside, something she had always wanted to do. A date appeared, March 29. It was three weeks away.

With persistence, she coaxed her attendant to turn through the yellow pages of a phone book under churches. Her eyesight was poor, but one of the churches seemed to glow off the page. The nurse attending her called the pastor for her, Scott Emerson. Since Marlene's speech was slurred, he thought she was drunk or making prank phone calls. But she began describing the inside of his church to him, and he listened. He arranged for Marlene to be brought to his church on March 29, and though they had never witnessed a miracle before, he and seven others gathered to pray for Marlene's healing.

Pastor Emerson prayed a simple prayer that God would heal Marlene from the top of her head to the soles of her feet. Afterward, he leaned down to ask Marlene if she would like to try to stand up in faith. She nodded yes. She was unbuckled, then unstrapped, and her feet were lifted from the footrests and placed on the floor. And when they touched the floor, for the first time she could *feel* them.

Marlene struggled to lift herself upright and began to walk! Awkwardly at first, then stronger, more confidently. Her pants were too big, and she had to hold them up as she began jogging around the sanctuary! As she did, her eyes began to burn, and she took off her thick glasses and had perfect vision. And her speech cleared. She was perfectly healed by God!

They all loaded up and went for ice cream. She had never held her own ice-cream cone before. Her therapist was at the parlor and could not believe the sight.

When Marlene walked back into the rehab unit that night, her doctors and nurses were dumbfounded. They asked her to stay another day to meet with a panel of doctors. And when she entered their room, they stood in applause. "Praise God!" one exclaimed.

Marlene drove up almost two hours to meet with us, pray and encourage us. She was as lovely, humble and genuine in person as on the phone. Much of my family made a whirlwind trip to be with us that night, including my parents, my brother and my sister. We prayed for Allen and my dad with a great deal of antici-pation. We were hoping they would be healed at our small prayer meeting, as Marlene had been. We took a camcorder along, just in case. We didn't know just how to end the evening, and it trailed off awkwardly, with disappointed good-byes.

Marlene drove home that night, refusing any mileage reim-bursement or fuss. It was so cool to meet a miracle. I loved her kind heart and simple love for God. Though she traveled some around the country to share her testimony, she was completely unfazed and unspoiled by the attention she got after her special touch from God. She lives a quiet life tending flowers at her shop and riding her bike through the warm, green Missouri countryside.

Allen and I were both a little down as we settled into bed that night. Meeting Marlene had been such a pick-me-up, but at the same time, it was a grim reminder that Allen was *not* healed. Many of our friends worried about us being disappointed and even questioned whether we should just accept things the way they were already and give up hoping for something more this side of heaven.

"I'm disappointed every time I pray," I would confess to them. "Should I stop praying?"

Accepting things the way they were or hoping for a healing didn't change our present situation one bit; it was just as difficult and heart-wrenching either way. But at least hoping in God seemed like what the Bible said we should do and carried with it the chance of a brighter future. The other option, resignation, seemed to assure our fate.

Soon after our visit with Marlene, I drove downtown and noticed a plaque in a storefront window. It said, "Life isn't about waiting for the storm to pass. It's about learning to dance in the rain" (author unknown).

It was a good quote and I agreed with it, mostly, but I would have said, "Life is about dancing in the rain until the storm passes." Along with that, 1 Timothy 6:6 sprang to mind, "Godliness with contentment is great gain." It seemed to me that contentment wasn't at odds with hope and faith, but rather was the by-product of them.

One dear friend, a professor, wrote to ask how I was doing. "You are like the child you see in pictures after a tornado rips through town. The child is sitting on a pile of sticks that once was home and playing in the rubble."

His remark made me feel good, even though I wasn't totally sure it was meant as a compliment. Allen, Lils and I did manage to have a pretty good time in spite of things. Lils and I liked to play with Allen's stuff when he wasn't using it—I'd putt around in his power chair for amusement when he was in bed. (He's a better driver than I am; I've already put several garfs in the wall.)

Lily had also found alternative uses for his other equipment—the lift that got him in and out of bed was a zip line. She could really fly on it. And his exercise bike was a planet in outer space for all her plastic bobble-head animals. My favorite thing was to see the way she would ride on the back of her dad's Jazzy 600 as he drove extra fast. She'd put her feet on the rear axle, hang on to the handlebars and squeal!

But the whole quadriplegia thing wasn't always a bowl of cherries. It had rocked our family dynamics like a tsunami. No area of our lives was untouched. Perhaps the greatest single threat to our marital bliss was not that we had an unsettling disability thrown our way. It wasn't even the financial drain of endless medical expenses. It was the fact that I was doing the driving.

I was a pretty bad driver to start with, but after trading in my small red car for a clunky minivan, I could really invoke terror on the roadways. Allen was so observant. He had always used great caution on the road, and now he was strapped in helplessly just a few feet behind me. He watched with panicked horror as I wove us through hapless hazards.

I made a wrong but familiar turn, and when we realized where I had taken us, it was as though someone turned on our tear ducts full blast.

Allen reminisced, "This is the same road we took when we returned the U-HAUL the day we moved to Rolla!"

Not the type of statement that would normally reduce two almost well-adjusted adults into weepy, slobbery messes, but I'm pretty sure that everyone we passed by on the road that day would have sworn we were listening to Karen Carpenter on the radio. Weird stuff just got to us at times. That day all it took was thinking about that time when we had come to town with such fresh excitement and hope, not knowing everything that might lie ahead, but willing to follow God wherever . . .

In the course of all our marital readjustments after the accident, I attended the wedding of a couple of just-outta-college kids. It was predictable in all its particulars: fancy hairdos, ill-fitting dresses, nervous giggles, slick vows. And I cried then, too, knowing that no matter how heartfelt their words, those poor kids didn't have any idea what those vows really meant and how hard it could become to live them well.

During their ceremony, I thought about how our wedding vows had glossed over much of what they had come to entail. (Don't get me started on booger rockets. I'll spare you the details.) Even before the accident, Allen had hung with me through laundry foibles, socks that never matched, "creative" checkbook ledgers and endless mountains of frozen dinners. Marriage sure wasn't what we thought it would be. I guess that becomes evident from the get-go. But marriage now seemed to me like a masterpiece in progress.

When I drew or painted, I was always embarrassed when someone would peek over my shoulder at a half-done sketch. It looked terrible in the middle as I erased and reworked and transferred my messy ideas onto a page in all kinds of disorder. I could envision in my mind where I was going with it all, but it looked like a wreck until the final pieces were in place. (And sometimes it looked like a wreck even then.) In the same way, our early years of marriage were a struggle, and then they were just a reckless spin of self-serving misdirection. Not terrible years between us—just a time full of a whole lot of selfishness and ambition as we chased careers, acting like two planets, each in their own orbit, that bumped into each other periodically. After that came the sleepless nights with a baby who required most of our focus. And just when we took a deep breath, thinking we were getting the whole picture figured out, life threw this curve with the accident . . .

When I took a break from my pontificating and came back to the wedding scene in front of me, I started laughing because when the preacher said, "You may kiss the bride," it actually looked as if the groom were going to eat that poor girl's face off. I didn't attend the reception afterward. I didn't even stay for the rice toss. I snuck straight home to be with my family, and that was exactly where I wanted to be.

12

VALUABLE RUINS

hey, doesn't Moses look like that one guy from the biography we watched the other night?" I asked as we turned on a movie about the children of Israel while I prepped Allen for bed. "With suspiciously well-groomed eyebrows," I noted.

"Have you ever noticed he and Moses are never in a room at the same time?" Allen teased, getting more mileage out of his standard Clark Kent joke.

Even though the movie wasn't really that well done, we had a good time watching it. The Amalekites were wearing disturbing cone-shaped metal hats on their heads.

"Guys, Grandma called and she wants her colanders back," I chided the screen.

"Look, it was the year of the staff," Allen jumped in as a battle scene drew near, showing people with long sticks in hand. "Moses had one, so everyone wanted one!"

Allen was approaching the one-year mark, a time limit the doctors had warned us about. Generally, it could mean an end to any further returning function. Allen had become more stable in his trunk, and movement in his arms had become more fluid and natural. However, there wasn't much else to report.

He did have a lot more feeling, but most of the new sensation was painful. In fact, the feeling in his armpits had become so bothersome that he was always asking me to undo the two lateral braces that fit under his arms and helped him sit up straight in his wheelchair. This request came at least a dozen times a day, and now even during the night, though he was in bed at the time. Just when I got snoozing good one night, I heard Allen talking in his sleep, so I unhappily dragged out from under a mountain of covers. I'd been out so heavily that I hadn't noticed I was sweating like a huge, round man at a monster truck rally in the middle of August.

"Chrissy, can you undo my laterals?" Allen asked. The laterals were nowhere in sight, mind you, since he was in his bed, not in his wheelchair. Baffled by what to do for him, I just said "Click" as I touched under each armpit. He said "Thanks" and trailed back off into a deeper sleep.

The next morning, we removed the pesky laterals from his wheelchair altogether, which seemed like an improvement until I went downstairs to carry something to the storage room. Allen sat next to a desk in our living room, talking on the phone with one of our neighbors. When I came upstairs from the basement, his head and shoulders were squarely resting on the desk, off to his right side! He was still talking on the phone like nothing had happened. The conversation had not skipped a beat, even when he had leaned over too far for something, and . . . whoops.

I sat him back upright, we smiled big at one another and he just went right on talking on the phone. When I was sure he was steady, I drove across town to pick Lils up from preschool. We watched as a caterpillar slowly inched across the well-traveled thoroughfare. I stopped the car, got out and moved him to a grassy place where he would stand a chance. It wasn't that I had a penchant for creepy crawlers, but I was rooting for him. The little guy had a butterfly in him.

"It's that way for God, I'll bet," I preached in the direction of the backseat. "He isn't put off at all by our smallness and yuck, but instead sees something inside of us, some potential worth salvaging, something maybe lovely even."

I tried to make it a teachable moment for Lils, who was heavily engrossed in some plastic green army guys, but she didn't say much other than that we should name the caterpillar Tony.

Going through a drive-thru to take home lunch, I rehearsed chapters from Matthew for Lily as we waited for our order. The first eight or nine chapters were familiar from childhood and came along easily, but by the time I got up to chapters 10, 11, 12 . . . I was struggling.

Finally, it was our turn. I drove up to the window and paid with a card. The lady at the window disappeared for a moment, and then reappeared with my card. I put it away in my wallet. Our order seemed to be taking longer than usual. The lady reappeared at the window, smiled a goofy smile and disappeared again. I continued on in Matthew. A few minutes passed, and she was back again. We smiled at each other awkwardly. The line of cars behind me grew. Six cars. Then eight. Again she came, more frazzled-looking and confused. Then, to my horror, I looked down to see my bag of food on the seat next to me. She had given it to me when she had returned my credit card!

When I got home, nothing in our bag was even sort of close to what we ordered. I guess the worker could have used a little more time after all. When we sorted through things, I commented, "Wow, you don't really put in an order at that place. More like you make a suggestion."

Lily offered to pray because she knew it would go faster and she could dive right in to a roll-up that was "slobbering" with cheese (her word choice).

Some things Allen could feed himself with a bent fork that fit snugly into a cuff on his hand. A chili-cheese burrito wasn't one of those things, so I held it for him while he took one painstakingly messy bite after another. A lot of times when I fed Allen, I would get bored holding stuff for him. There aren't too many things more boring than waiting for someone to chew, so I found myself eating half of his food to make it go faster. (This hardly ever happened when he was eating lentils or broccoli.) He was always good-natured about it. He couldn't really feel when he was hungry anymore. It was all sort of guesswork.

It bothered Allen that Lily might not remember what things had been like before the accident, when he was walking. Often over meals or before bed, he'd tell her stories of things we'd all done together. Whenever I thought about how nice things had been, I got saddish, so I avoided all such conversations. When people asked if things were getting easier with the passing of time, I said yes, things were easier. But truthfully, I think things got easier only because we were forgetting what life was like before. Rolling up our sleeves and focusing on the work at hand seemed good therapy.

I was glad the phone rang to break up all the sentimental mush going on over lunch. The "glorious past" was still just too much for me to wade into. On the line was one of the girls who had graduated from our campus ministry a few years prior. She was stopping through town and wanted to get together for coffee. She was a beautiful girl, a successful engineer, and I looked forward to seeing her again.

Rolla didn't have much to offer in the way of trendy cafés, but we met at a well-liked restaurant near campus and sat at a small table along the edge, near windows. All around us, people were engrossed in laptop computers and lattes, and a few read newspapers. In her open way, this girl began to pour out what was on her heart. She had quit her job and loaded up everything she had in a car, and now she was driving around visiting old friends.

It didn't seem that out of the ordinary to me because she didn't have any attachments and lots of our students took cool road trips, even internationally, just because they could. But her situation was different, and even though she wasn't exactly sure where she was going, she was definitely headed away from something. I didn't probe, but she freely continued her story. Her boss had forced himself on her, and she was devastated. He quit. She quit. And she was left trying to sort out dozens of questions about life, tragedy and God.

I would have thought myself prepared for a conversation like this, having sat through a few crisis counseling classes in college. But I didn't know what to say. I should have reached across the table and hugged her good. Instead, I started stirring my hot chocolate frantically, as though my single purpose in life was to wield that tiny plastic straw with the determination, speed and proficiency of an Olympic medalist. I gave her a weird, pained half smile, as if to say, "I'm so sorry." Then the conversation halted in an awkward pause.

I pulled my worn Bible from my purse in an effort to be Bibley. I shared dozens of verses that had helped to pull me through. I'm sure it all sounded canned at first, but as the conversation eased into a more natural flow—and I promise this is true—we both began to swap stories about the goodness of God and how crazy-merciful He had been to us in the midst of our catastrophes. How close He had dared to brush in our grief-stricken hours. Of course, there were periods when both of us, in our respective torments, had been waist-deep in manure-thick doubts. But we couldn't, either one of us, deny God's presence right there beside us in the muck.

We agreed that even though no one likes to go through such things or suffer losses, anytime you get more of God, it's a mega-consolation. When you lose everything and you're down-and-out desperate, you get Jesus for a gift. Nice.

It was that way for Stephen, martyred in the book of Acts. He was serving, preaching and obeying the Lord when people picked up big rocks to throw at him. God didn't whisk him out of that situation. But Stephen got to see Jesus, and he was excited about it. "Look!" he shouted to the angry, rock-pitching people, "Can you *see* that?!"

We went for a ride in the car that had become my friend's mobile apartment. We were absorbed in our conversation so completely by then that I found myself stomping on the imaginary passenger brake pedal several times, worried that maybe she forgot she was driving. Our lives at present were different—hers was filled with freedom and uncertainties, while mine was filled with responsibilities that left me very little free time. But we talked about how we had found common ground—God's comfort in the middle of a fat, ugly mess. When we finally parted after a hug, she was on her way.

I squeezed Lily tightly when I got home and smiled because she was playing with the ugliest toy on earth. I'd once given her two quarters to spend at a flea market in Eldon, Iowa, the quaint river town that inspired Grant Wood's *American Gothic* painting. She fell in love with a small, filthy stuffed kitten with giant bug-eyes. It was from a discarded Happy Meal. I did all I could to dissuade her, even offering to add to her buying power so she could purchase a puzzle, a board game, a robot—*anything* else.

Nope. Two years later, she still treasured her stuffed kitten. That's her way. Lily loves stuff that looks like junk to me. Countless times she had rescued things out of the trash with a pained, how-could-you expression. I had even found my cast-off sketches hung carefully on the refrigerator in the place of greatest honor, just about three feet from the ground. I loved that about Lily. I buried my nose in her soft cheek.

Like most people I know, I don't like to keep broken stuff around. But I had never given it too much thought until our accident. Some people were goofed out by our brokenness. I think they didn't know what to say. Or seeing wheelchairs and stuff just made them feel so bad, they didn't know how to process it. Some of our friends didn't call as much, or seemed in a hurry to get away, or were just bored since we weren't really cool or fun or spontaneous anymore, especially not now. We had so little to offer, yet needed so much attention, and we always felt like a big, hairy spectacle.

One of my favorite passages is Isaiah 61:1–2, "The Spirit of the Sovereign LORD is on me, because the LORD has anointed me to preach good news to the poor. He has sent me to bind up the brokenhearted, to proclaim freedom for the captives and release from darkness for the prisoners, to proclaim the year of the LORD's favor."

These verses are a nice reminder to reach out to the broken, I'd thought as I highlighted them the summer before our life went nuts. And I liked that heart-stopping moment when Jesus read these verses to the Jews in the synagogue. And like an artist who pulls the veil off his work, a priceless sculpture, Jesus went on to say, "I'm the one."

But now what caught my attention was later in the passage, when the Lord called a motley crew of prisoners and the depressed and broken-down people "oaks of righteousness, a planting of the LORD for the display of his splendor" (verse 3).

God gave the lowly ones the task of rebuilding His flattened Kingdom. Not the people I would have picked for my task force, but if pressed, I would have to admit that those I consider the heart and soul of our church are those who have waded through dark, dark times. It seemed Lils wasn't the only one to cherish the homely. I was getting the idea that God Himself found great value in those the world deemed ruined.

13

Getting Places

I was sitting uncomfortably in the dentist's chair. Animal
Planet was on TV, and I watched with horror as a boa constrictor
gobbled down an antelope. Then in a flood of remorse, the snake
barfed it back up again. Maybe it needed salt and pepper? Maybe
he needed to fit into his tight jeans for speed-dating night? Maybe
the animal kingdom has eating disorders?

I was awaiting a gum graft since I'd been brushing my teeth side
to side instead of in small circles, too hard, too much. Since I was
brushing Allen's teeth a lot these days, he complained, "Great,
pretty soon I'll need one, too."

The periodontist came chairside. He was wearing muddy crocs,
as if he were just in from milking a cow and patching a barbwire
fence. My heart was beating violently in my chest, and my fingers
had a strangle grip on the armrests. He told me he'd never had a

patient so nervous. Having been recognized with such a distinction made me more nervous. He cracked jokes all through the procedure. I'm not sure which was worse, the procedure or his jokes.

"How did it go?" Allen asked when I got home.

"Imagine skinning the leather from a football—only it isn't a football, it's the roof of your mouth," I complained as I sat down at the piano. To be dumb, I began plunking out songs from *Mad Max Beyond Thunderdome*. I'd never actually seen that movie, but the thought of it made me laugh, probably because I was heavily medicated.

This inspired Allen to play his picks of really nutty eighties songs from iTunes at top volume, and we had a wacky-song war.

As the Novocain wore off, my mood sobered. I took a break from the sing-along and read in my Bible about the prophet Elijah. It was a familiar passage, but it revealed an unexpected twist at the end that I hadn't remembered. Like every good story, it had a bad guy, King Ahab, and his partner in crime, Queen Jezebel, who had an almost comic-book villainy. They were the kind of folks who would kill a nice guy (Naboth) just because they wanted his vineyard. Yup, they liked grapes *that* much.

Before that crime, even, God sent Elijah to tell them off because they loved-loved idols. Elijah prayed God would stop the rain for a bit, even though it would make his own life unpleasant and complicated. God thought it was a good idea, and it got people's attention—the Empirical Evils were duly annoyed. After a while, God sent Elijah back to them, challenging the prophets of Baal to a showdown. Elijah exhibited incredible faith and confidence that God would show up and fry his sacrifice, leaving the fake-god wannabes looking rather, well, silly.

The prophets of Baal were humiliated, and then their day got worse. They were slaughtered. Elijah told the king to get home or the rain would ruin his picnic. Rain? It hadn't rained in over three years.

Just when I thought Elijah had the market on cockiness and every bit of well-deserved assurance, he sat down on Mount Carmel, his head buried between his knees. Too nervous to look at the sky himself, he asked his trusty servant for a weather report. Anything? Nothing.

He asked again and again, each time with increasing anxiety. Seven times he asked. Nothing. Finally, a teeny, tiny cloud no bigger than a man's hand appears. Aaaah. I felt his relief. He ran down the mountain, offered Ahab a final jab and made his way into the desert, where he collapsed in utter despair.

I'm not sure what it's like to be a prophet. Reading the passage, it seemed like not a good life to me, but if I were guessing about what prophet types would think of as a crowning moment, Elijah's Mount Carmel experience would be it. I'm not sure why he despaired, but I was relieved when I saw a Bible guy filled with the kind of twisted complexities I recognize in my own fusspot of emotions. Confidence in God, with a great deal of perspiration. Trust, victory, despair. And how sometimes, even on the heels of witnessing God's extraordinary stuff, I longed to see just the smallest glimmer of promise to dare me to keep believing.

As our friends vacationed in great places, enjoyed terrific job success or brought home sweet new babies, I tallied up our minuses and couldn't help but think, *You know, our life isn't really going so well.* We wanted awesome vacations. We wanted cool jobs. We wanted babies. *Bring on babies!* Our doctor told us it was possible with some fiddling. But even if we tried it or adopted or whatever, how on earth would we manage to care for a new little one? As it was, our beta's fish tank looked like a bowl of chunky stew.

I was trying to "keep the faith," "keep my chin up" and all those other feel-good catchphrases. Down deep, though, I felt hurt that my life was going so poorly when the very God of the universe had seemed so close a friend.

Mostly, I punished myself with doubts like, *What am I doing wrong here? Is God totally upset with something in my life? Do we have too much stuff? Am I not giving enough to the poor? Am I not telling people about Him enough? Am I ignoring a command somewhere? Am I too wrapped up in this world? Why doesn't He like me anymore?*

It sounds extreme, but you know how those doubts creep in and get the better of you? I even agonized on occasion, *Gracious! Am I even saved?* I was positive that the Bible and all its promises were true, but my prayers felt powerless! That seemed a really huge problem.

Before the accident, I often prayed with a small roomful of people from church once or twice a week. Sometimes afterward, we'd all go out for lunch together. On a Tuesday when I knew they were meeting, I went to pray with them again. It was the first time I'd gone since the accident. I asked Allen to join me, but he had a meeting to attend.

I think the old gang was initially happy to see me, but as soon as I opened my mouth to pray, I fear I majorly bummed out the Prayer Zone. I prayed something terribly sad, blabbing out the deepest darkness in me. Something like, "God, how will You ever work this out? I have no idea how something smashed into smithereens can ever be put back together, whole again. I kind of thought things were different between us, that we were friends. Why didn't You stop this from happening or warn me? I've loved You from my kid years. I'm coming to ask You to please have mercy on my family. Even if You didn't like me, I would still love You. And even though

You aren't really answering my prayers right now, I still want You for my God. I wouldn't last a second without You."

We were all overdosing on hankies as they shared my monster truckload of "Woe Is Me!" Most days I was fine. Some days, I dare say, were even good. But whenever something reminded me of our old ways, or when I saw a look in Allen's face as though he were sad, or if I heard Lils pray in faith, all my togetherness took a long hike to an unknown destination.

Lily had her bags packed and waiting by the door for the moment her dad was healed. She wanted to go places—to Grandma's house, to the beach, to Disneyland.

"Mom, the Bible says if we believe it will happen, our prayers will come true, right? So it has to happen, right?" she inquired.

"Yes, honey," I reassured her, throwing caution to the wind. I wasn't about to throw a wet blanket on her confidence or be the one to unpack those bags. They were a sort of monument to her beautiful, expectant faith. So I vacuumed and tidied around the little pink suitcase, set stuff around it, but never moved it.

I knew deep down that even if Allen were healed, we'd still carry this awful thing, like the scar I have from surgery years ago that looks as if the surgeon were wearing dark, oversized clown sunglasses when she took the scalpel in her hand. What I mean is that things could never be the old fun and carefree way again for us. It's as if we've been marinated in a powerful punch of sobriety, altering the flavor of things for good. I thought of Job, even at the end of the ordeal. His health and life were restored, but how he must have grieved for the children he'd lost and all the baggage he now had to lug along. I tried not to explore that kind of thinking too much.

It seemed our moods and our lives in general were like the stock market, given to sharp downturns and spirals, but meant to be endured for the long haul, with great strides and recoveries. There were days, I'm sure, that investors felt like gouging the stock ticker off the screens of their laptops and TVs with meat forks, but those times called for temperance, patience and optimism. Easier said than done.

We took Allen back to Columbia for fourteen more days of rehab. His neurologist called it a one-year "tune-up" to capitalize on any gains Allen had made and address any problems. Insurance consented. We rarely made it out of town, so on the way we surprised Lily with a trip to the food mecca of childhood—Chuck E. Cheese. There, surrounded by cheap thrills, euphoric children and a guy dressed in a huge cartoon mouse costume, Allen and I sat weeping—a sight I'm sure they don't often see at Chuck E. Cheese. We laughed through watery eyes at the irony. I'm not totally sure just what got us so choked up, but I think we were grieving Lily's weird new childhood and how we were all three kind of missing out on what we had hoped it would be.

Checking Allen back into Rusk Rehabilitation Center was like arriving for the first day of summer camp. His therapists and nurses were all so glad to see him again. There were hugs and smiles and people circling around. Once we got him bundled in for the night, I felt sad that our family would be separated again. I took Allen's hand in mine while we said our good-byes, and I noticed myself stroking his hand softly even though he couldn't feel it. I didn't stop even when I realized what I was doing. I knew it still meant something, although he wasn't able to feel it physically.

The halls were getting dark as visiting hours ended. Seeing Allen back in that hospital bed made me feel guilty all over again that I'd come out of the accident so well. After kisses, Lily and I headed off to a nearby hotel. I couldn't begin to imagine what it might be like to sleep all through the night without being up and down a half-dozen times.

Lily fell right asleep, but I turned and fussed, trying to get comfortable. My head was at a 90-degree angle, resting on the rock-hard hotel pillow ball. (How do hotels manage to find such bad pillows? It must be included in Hotel Training 101, along with making sure housekeeping bangs on the door at the exact moment that you step out of the shower.)

When finally I nodded off, I dreamed of a beautiful house, huge but cottagelike in its quaintness, cut from a single stone. It was settled in the woods, with flowers everywhere and a clear blue stream running along one side. The green grass looked as though it had been digitally altered, turning the color saturation way up until it looked unnaturally brilliant.

That stream is way too close to the house, I thought. *People don't build houses so close to the water. And look how clear blue it is!* I analyzed the scene right in the midst of my dream. What I liked best about the tan stone house was the rounded cornice over each window and door frame. There were no actual doors or windows, only frames.

Somehow, in my sleep I thought, *Oh, this is a house in heaven.* When I woke up at the dream's end, I realized that God is always trying to remind us that the uglier this world gets, the more we should keep working toward heaven, where He has a home for us.

I was grateful for the reminder, but often it was impossible for me to grasp or imagine a real life that began at the end of this one. In that sense, even thoughts of heaven were not always comforting. I found myself hoping that God cared about this wreck of a life, too, and I knew He did. He promised to care about flower-speckled, grassy fields and even sparrows (though they leave white, splotchy messes all over our deck and car windows).

I knew Jesus was the exact representation of God, and He never missed an opportunity to spring into action when folks were in need of compassion. He even cared about people's rumbling stomachs when He preached long and they missed a few meals.

Lily and I made a whirlwind trip home over the weekend, while Allen was still in rehab. We had promised to host a garage sale with our neighbors, and we had obligations at church as well. I knew our garage situation was dire when I had to vacuum cobwebs off the shop vac before using it to suck up bugs in various stages of decomposition from the windowsills and corners.

After working tirelessly to clean the garage, I sorted and tagged a mountain of old, unwanted things. Then I greeted droves of eager townspeople who anxiously rifled through the folded piles I'd so neatly stacked. Finally, after I loaded up and delivered armfuls of unsold stuff to charity, I collected the usual eight dollars in change we had earned. Too exhausted to cook, we quickly spent it on take-out food.

It seemed like we were in that kind of rut all the way around. It was so exhausting and hard just for us to be alive and going while making pocket-sized contributions to anything truly valuable. Allen found this frustration overwhelming as well.

I prayed, "God, I don't have anything to offer You. Just a lot of being on super empty. I'm anxious to unload our mess because I have absolutely no idea what to do with it. Still, it seems like a perfectly terrible thing to offer a King. There were times in my life when I felt so much more valuable. Like maybe I could offer You my life and that would mean something. But *this*? You want *this* wreck? The Bible says what You want is a broken spirit. That's just what I happen to have. So please, Lord, take every part of my life. If there is any way it can be any good to You, count me in. I love You, Lord. You mean absolutely everything to me."

I had in mind that God was getting us someplace, that He was working on us. And God always did seem to take longer than people thought He should. Poor Noah, after working on his boat nearly one hundred years in the midst of merciless heckling, had to then sit in it with a lot of stinky animals for a whole week before the first raindrop fell. It is easy in hindsight to see that the rain delay showed God's huge mercy for all those who would soon be swimming, but I can't imagine Noah's torment.

I wondered if maybe we weren't waiting on God as much as He was waiting on us. I was pretty sure He wasn't trying to teach me how to bathe someone and shave his whiskers, how to hold someone's spoon without spilling cereal all over him (although that was proving to be a challenge), how to dispense medicine or even perform simple nursing tasks.

God was clanking away at the very heart of me in a manner that seemed most unpleasant. *Maybe if I get with the program and learn the stuff—whatever it is—we can get on with the next thing?* I reasoned.

We had received a newsletter from a missionary whose name I can't mention since he needs to be kept safe. One story in the newsletter really got to me, and I highlighted a sentence, clipped out the paragraph and hung it on our refrigerator. It told about a girl who had come to Jesus, gone on to study at seminary and then returned to lead worship at the ministry that had discipled her. "She is today what she decided upon ten years ago" was the line that hit me squarely.

I wanted to become a better person, bloom in trial, get somewhere in ten years and all that, too. But I was too tired to figure out how and where.

14

DESPERATE MEASURES

It was day four of our Cheez Whiz binge. My brother's family was visiting, and we'd been eating a lot of overprocessed cheese. Everyone was standing around, nachos in hand, laughing and feeling good while I was helping Allen get hooked up to some exercise equipment.

Because of people's generosity, Allen had been able to purchase an FES cycle to continue therapy at home, since insurance had waved good-bye to all other physical therapy options. The FES or Functional Electronic Stimulation system used electrodes to create movement in his legs that would cycle an exercise bike.

It took a long time to strap him up, but every other day he would ride a full hour, almost thirteen miles, on the bike. It didn't take long before his atrophied legs began to beef up again and his overall health began to improve. But on this morning, while on the bike, he pushed himself too far.

"I can't breathe," he complained.

"In a bad way?" I asked half-jokingly as I hurried close.

"Grab a trash can," he said, nauseated, "and stop the bike!" Then, seeing how close he was to breaking his personal record for distance, he said, "Wait, no, don't stop it yet." Then he waffled, "Stop the bike!"

By this time I had already stopped it and was unstrapping his legs, but he had no idea. "Go ahead and stop the bike," he repeated weakly.

"I already did, honey," I whispered, suddenly sober as I unfastened the last strap. I touched his face. He was burning up, so I took his temperature—over 104 degrees! We called an ambulance.

Allen was 100 percent sure he was dying. Every movement, every word he spoke sent "electric" jolts up his legs and through the rest of his body. Weird neurological sensations weren't uncommon for his condition, but this was different. He felt he was going into shock. In spite of the discomfort, he confessed his past mistakes. He tried to coach me in finance. He asked for prayer.

My family and I huddled around him, praying while we waited impatiently for the ambulance to arrive. We were all in a panic. Not knowing exactly what to do, my sister-in-law, who still had some wits about her, offered him the fix-all, a drink of cold water.

Lily was so involved in playing with her cousin that I don't think she worried much when the ambulance backed up our driveway. I was glad she was distracted and that she didn't ask the paramedics to sound the horn or give her a ride around the block. Once Allen was loaded, I raced close behind the flashing ambulance and rushed inside the ER, where everything else seemed to move in slow motion. The ER staff assigned Allen a room and packed him in cool rags. It was hours before his temperature came down.

Before Lily was born, I had volunteered in this hospital for years. I knew my way around, familiar with all the nooks and crannies. But it seemed a different place altogether—a lot less fun—when we needed to be here. They had brought us into *this* very emergency room that traumatic, sunny August day. That day, I had come in with a full-on concussion. Bedecked in the usual unflattering gown in one of these exam rooms, I had been doing and saying who knows what, in some kind of stupor.

Now back again because of Allen's condition, I was pressing my memory as hard as I could to recall the awful morning this whole thing with us began. I even snooped through the hallway, hoping something would trigger my memory. It was still lost, though, out of reach in that thick ocean of head-thumping blankness that descended on me after the accident.

As I paced the halls one direction, then another, scouting for clues, my mouth moved in a sloppy rendition of Luke 18:7–8, verses that wrap up the parable of a persistent widow who won a favorable ruling from a crotchety judge by driving him totally nuts with her importunity. "Will not God bring about justice for his chosen ones, who cry out to him day and night? . . . He will see that they get justice, and quickly!" I said it over and over again, twenty, thirty times, and when I felt doubt creeping in, I repeated it a bit more audibly.

I snuck back into Allen's room just as a nervous technician, still wet behind the ears, came to X-ray Allen's chest.

"Try not to move," the boy said anxiously.

"It's not often people say that to a quad," Allen joked. His banter showed he was beginning to feel some better.

After Allen's condition stabilized several hours later, they sent us home, still unsure what had happened or what to tell us. After that, Allen was unable to tolerate almost any form of exercise, and the months that followed were a frustrating medical maze as doctors tried to figure out exactly what was wrong. Several more nerve-wracking visits to the ER indicated that Allen's health was more delicate than ever.

One time at about 2:00 in the morning, Allen complained of a pounding headache. His blood pressure, which was almost always frightfully low, was 200 on top. Once again we called an ambulance. By the time the paramedics arrived, Allen's blood pressure seemed to be dropping, so we sent them on their way. The ambulance was barely out of the driveway when I saw that Allen's capillaries were bursting and he was passing blood. We prayed, and things improved dramatically. His blood pressure stabilized, things cleared up and Allen slept soundly through the rest of the night.

Then came a pressure ulcer that had him laid up in bed for almost three weeks, staring at one wall and then the other. "I'm going to take a quick shower," I said one day, bored by the bedroom scenery we were growing so accustomed to.

"I'm going to lie here really, really still," he replied halfheartedly.

With every passing day, Allen's excruciating pain seemed to increase. Weakened, he was able to tolerate less and less time sitting up. Even though family visited frequently and our church friends helped constantly, there were times like these when we felt completely overwhelmed and alone. We knew we had to exhaust all possibilities when it came to Allen being healed.

A couple from Namibia, Africa, had invited us to a small prayer meeting at a hotel in Kansas City. They were full of faith for healing and had personally witnessed many miracles. Allen felt up to traveling at the time, so even though we didn't know how we'd manage it, we loaded up for a scary, burdensome road trip.

The van ride was actually full of fun and hope. A loud growl echoed as I accidentally crossed over the centerline.

"Does someone have gas?" Lily joked as she puttered in back with her action figures.

"That would give new meaning to *rumble strip*," I quipped under my breath.

As we drove through a small town, we passed a huddled group of teenagers smoking.

"Is smoking cigarettes against the Ten Commandments, Mom?" Lily asked earnestly.

"No," I said, "but the Bible says God's Holy Spirit lives inside our bodies, so we should take good care of them."

"I hope the Holy Spirit likes ice cream," she contemplated. We laughed.

And we dreamed about whether or not Allen would be the one driving home.

The metropolitan traffic was enough in itself to give me tumors, without all the other stresses. I am not a city person. Good friends graciously led us into town to ease the burden. It was a relief when we pulled off the interstate and into the parking lot of the hotel in which we'd stay. It was right where the prayer meeting would take place.

We were a parade, the three of us, juggling bags and weird cushions and other mysterious medical stuff into the lavish hotel. The lady behind the desk was curt, and at once I felt aged and hideous, which called into question all of my abilities to be charming. Our room was up several floors, coldish and fancy in an outdated sort of way. But it was good to be closed up tight and cozy, able to breathe—even though the air seemed stale and foreign and not at all natural like the wholesome Iowa air I'd grown up with.

Transferring Allen in and out of bed was next to impossible. At home, we used a lift. "You're going to break my neck again!" he complained as I grunted and struggled. We were relieved when he was finally situated without incident.

I called down to the front desk in my most agreeable, friendly way with what must have been a common question. Still, the desk clerk seemed frosty. I soon found another excuse to call down, because I need people to like me.

"Two questions," I began affably. "First, is there a trick to getting this microwave to work? I can't figure it out. And secondly, my husband is wondering if you have any Pepto-Bismol tablets down there by chance? Perhaps in a vending machine? I guess he doesn't hold high hopes for this TV dinner . . ." I laughed.

The desk clerk answered in cyborg fashion, efficient but distant.

You'd think I would have my hands full with an ailing, quadriplegic husband and our life's dreams unraveling at the seams. You'd think I would have little time or energy to care about whether or not I was well liked by a hotel hostess I would never see again. You'd think . . .

But somewhere in the story of my efforts with the desk clerk was the story of my dogged pursuit to win God's favor. It was so difficult in the midst of things to dare to think He liked me.

"Am I noncute? Hideously repulsive? Uncharming?" I asked Allen insecurely. "Not hip? Annoying? Unlikable?"

"You're the hottest fifty-year-old I know," Allen teased.

Little comfort since I was in my thirties at the time. And then he smiled and said some sweet, affirming, awesome stuff.

Lily fell asleep uncharacteristically early. I balled up in a dim corner with my Bible. "Do you think it's bad that I have a chocolate chip/walnut cookie recipe scribbled in here?" I asked Allen as I leafed through the pages of my prayer journal.

"Really? Walnuts?" Allen was unimpressed.

I impressed myself by getting completely dressed and ready for bed without setting down my sandwich once. I called it a "pickle-wich" because I like tons of pickles. And when it was gone, I snuggled in next to Allen. It was one of the few nights we could sleep in the same bed since he stayed in a thin hospital bed at home. The hospital bed made it tons easier on me to turn him, get him comfy and adjusted, get his clothes changed and other practical stuff, but it sure was a gigantic bummer. However, half the time it was of little consequence. He lived with such discomfort that any little touch hurt. But we both missed hugs and cuddling so much that sometimes he welcomed mush, even though it was painful.

"Do these sheets smell like tacos to you?" I asked.

I was half-expecting him to suggest another call to the front desk. "Oh, I cut onions at lunch," I remembered, and I trailed off to sleep, exhausted by all the travel and phone calls.

The next morning, I woke early and tried to rehearse all the verses I'd been coaching myself with that taught the rewards of faith in prayer. "Anyone who has faith in me will do what I have been doing. He will do even greater things than these, because I am going to the Father. And I will do whatever you ask in my name, so that the Son may bring glory to the Father. You may ask me for anything in my name, and I will do it" (John 14:12–14).

"It does say *anyone*," I noted as I got Allen dressed and ready. Then Lily. I ran a brush through my own hair, pulling it back in a rubber band, then changed my mind because with such sparse hair, it looked like a "rattail" from the eighties. My shirt, on the other hand, was now loaded with hair, as though I'd been hugging an Alaskan malamute.

When we were all three put together, we headed down to the meeting room and waited impatiently for the prayer service to begin. I had no idea how we'd keep Lils quiet through a service that was slated to last hours. I lugged a backpack loaded with snacks, books and toys. We sat quietly, nervously, on the back row, not knowing what to expect. I was sneaking into Lily's snacks, which brought disapproving looks from both husband and child.

Things began with worship. Relieved that I was familiar with all the songs, I sang out strong. And then some pastors spoke about all Jesus did for us and His desire to redeem us in every way. They hammered away at the notion that Jesus only took up the diseases and infirmities of those in Bible times.

Isaiah 53 was one pastor's main text, and he asked, "If we believe the rest of that chapter applies to us regarding our salvation, why do we write off the verses that explain His willingness to carry our sickness?"

And then came the gut-twisting moment. We walked up front, admitting how much we needed help. There were hands all about us, pleading with the Father on our behalf for an extra measure of grace. Everyone prayed long by anyone's standards. In a hot burst of panic, I realized I'd been so caught up in things, I'd completely lost track of Lily. Yet there she was, her little hands clasped firmly together, eyes squeezed tightly shut, praying with all her small might.

Before long, Lils and I were sitting on a bench at the edge of the parking lot, next to Allen in *that* chair. We were not utterly disappointed, really, but we felt bedraggled and deflated, like an untied balloon let loose. All at once it flies high and fast momentarily—before landing with a thump on the floor amongst all the hair balls, dirt and nail clippings.

I experienced the aching, nagging notion that said, "See, you set yourself up, chump!" I agreed with everything the pastors had taught us about God's desire to heal, body and soul. But sometimes ideas were great in theory, and while they worked out well for a few people, they just didn't play out for the majority. Kind of like the Diaper Genie or skinny jeans.

Please, God, don't let this be one of those things, I thought.

I think I was more disappointed than Allen. He had been a good sport about it all, but mostly came because I wanted to. Neither of us really knew for a fact whether or not we had been on the right track by coming, or if we were just rabbit trailing.

We loaded up and began the long trip home. Once again, our friends had offered to lead us back to Rolla since they were heading that direction themselves. I was happy to travel together since it was getting late and most of the driving would be after dark.

We were all spent, physically and emotionally. Lily wanted desperately to go to sleep, but she had dropped her pink, silky blankie on the floor of the van, out of reach. She pleaded with me to pull to the side of the road, but there was no shoulder. She begged to unlatch her seatbelt so she could reach down and get it, but I wanted her to stay safe. In exhaustion she wept and wept, and I felt that awful, heartsick pang that God knows full well when He has to say "wait" to His brokenhearted child.

When we got home and everyone was snug in bed, I settled into a steaming-hot bubble bath, as if to drown my sorrows. I ate a bowl of cucumbers and onions with a huge serving spoon as I soaked, and I did a good bit of sulking. A passage from Habakkuk 3:17–18 nagged at me. "Though the fig tree does not bud and there are no grapes on the vines, though the olive crop fails and the fields produce no food, though there are no sheep in the pen and no cattle in the stalls, yet I will rejoice in the LORD, I will be joyful in God my Savior."

Convicted, I tried dutifully to give thanks for at least one thing. The random thought came to mind that not everyone has a dad and mom praying for them, so I gave thanks for my parents. Then I added, "God, I don't understand any of this. Not a bit. I'm trying to trust You. I *know* You are good, and I'll never stop loving You . . ."

15

MIGHTY SEED

We'd been struggling along this way for two years now. Like grocery store produce, we'd been plucked too early, before we were ripe even. Now we felt officially withered and moldy. Always exhausted, my eyeballs felt like shriveled little pieces of dried-out cheese. It was getting harder and harder to fit in with the exuberant college students Allen worked with; they were so full of fun and life. We wondered how long to stick with it. His involvement had dwindled drastically already.

We were learning those hard lessons you hate to learn. Valuable, but painful. Like finding out the tough way that the much-pierced, tattooey, extremely huge guy on a Harley actually doesn't like to be called "Fatty."

One night Allen lay in bed in terrible pain—not the kind of pain that can be fixed. Just weird, inexplicable pain that comes from your nerves and spinal cord being mashed up. He asked me to pray for him, and I did. And then I opened my Bible to whatever it came to, which was 1 Peter chapters 4 and 5. One verse shocked me so much, I might have objected to it if it hadn't been God Himself saying it: "Therefore, since Christ suffered in his body, arm yourselves also with the same attitude, because he who has suffered in his body is done with sin. As a result, he does not live the rest of his earthly life for evil human desires, but rather for the will of God" (1 Peter 4:1–2).

The passage was like a personal note from God. It ended with a promise: "And the God of all grace, who called you to his eternal glory in Christ, after you have suffered a little while, will himself restore you and make you strong, firm and steadfast" (1 Peter 5:10). Reading the verses aloud was reminiscent of one of those dramatic movie moments—the lights soften, and sappy music begins to spin in the background so you know something significant is about to happen and you shouldn't take a popcorn break, whatever you do. Not that I was expecting something out of the ordinary to happen, but the verses just struck me that good.

Allen wanted the pain to stop, just as I would—just as anyone would. We tried whatever we could, confounded about why God would allow such a thing. But there was that whisper deep down, urging us that there is a value in suffering, which our culture hadn't understood or prepared us for. Maybe in an effort to distract him, I tried to be helpful, sermonizing about Jesus' suffering. How God's voice came booming out of heaven at Jesus' baptism: "Hey, I love this guy. I am pleased with this guy. He's My boy." No question where He stood with God. Yet three years later, Jesus was wrestling with God's will in a garden on the eve of His death.

"Isn't there some other way, God?" Jesus agonized. Unthinkable that God's most prized and cherished Son should be wiping off loogies and nursing the punches of big jerks. That He should die in a terrible and humiliating way.

I referenced Hebrews 5:7–8, "While Jesus was here on earth, he offered prayers and pleadings, with a loud cry and tears, to the one who could rescue him from death. And God heard his prayers because of his deep reverence for God. Even though Jesus was God's Son, he learned obedience from the things he suffered" (NLT).

Even on the cross, Christ didn't shy away from suffering. He refused the wine mixed with gall, a primitive analgesic that the soldiers offer Him as He hung there. Unlike me—I grab the bottle of ibuprofen with lightning speed in my discomfort.

Allen bore my ramblings and didn't complain about my irritating need to try to spiritualize everything or downplay the misery of it all. Looking back, I sometimes wonder why he didn't lose his lunch over all my prolific preaching. I did it more for me, honestly. I needed to hear myself defending God's heroic goodness. Allen was already strides past me in his understanding of it.

As Allen lay awake all through that night, God worked a miracle in him in the midst of his suffering. There, in pain and sleeplessness, Allen gave thanks for every single person he could think of who had in some way helped or encouraged him through the course of his trial. He praised God for many hours, and in the morning there he was, a new man.

When I woke up, he said something like, "God told me . . ."

I have no idea what he said after that. I was stuck on the first part, dumbstruck. I think I made a poor joke like, "Who are you, and what have you done with my husband?" Or maybe I asked, "Should I check the yard for crop circles?"

It was really not like the Allen I knew to talk that way. It was wonderful to hear him talking about the Lord almost constantly, asking to pray many times a day and listening to the Bible on MP3 more and more. Allen was already a good man, serving well in ministry and long respected by everyone. But something profound had happened to him in the long hours of that night. There came awake in him a fire for God that had not been there before. And I came to realize that, though God doesn't cause tragedies such as ours to happen, he doesn't waste them, either.

It was a Sunday morning, and it gave me hope when I realized God was answering prayer more and better than I had asked. I'd been tirelessly praying for Allen's physical healing. Allen had once even heard me sleeptalking, uttering prayers for him and for Dad. But God was interested in wholeness, beginning with our hearts. God had in mind total redemption, working something of far greater significance than I could have imagined, whereas I'd been moping around because He hadn't yet granted us lesser things.

Meanwhile, Satan threw all sorts of trials our way to get us to buckle—hurtful happenings among friends, new waves of medical complications and excruciating pain. But God was supplying us with grace to meet each challenge, even though we'd rather have avoided them altogether.

One late afternoon, as I pulled the dross out of my flower bed, the weeds and dead vines that were frizzled out by the almost August, heavy sun, there came an outlandish peace at the realization of what God was working in us. I prayed, "God, I think I can trust You to do Your whole dealie here." And I contemplated the slight, flea-sized possibility that He really could work something good out of it all.

My Bible memory work had stalled out in the sixteenth chapter of Matthew. Every time I mowed the grass, I tried to recite everything I had learned. The neighbors were nearly certain I was mad, as I appeared to be talking to no one. Despite my best efforts, the chapters were getting jumbled, and I felt I couldn't possibly memorize another verse. And so I took a break and got jazzed up about another idea I had. I wanted to learn how to recite Isaiah 53:4–5 in Hebrew. Even though I knew it was a silly notion, I thought maybe Hebrew was "God's language," and it seemed cool to me at that particular moment to try speaking it.

I spent a whole afternoon so engrossed in my plan that I felt a bit guilty for neglecting my family. I got annoyed when they distracted me with the necessary things that came up, such as, "Hey, Mom, can you help me find that blue plastic swamp creature?" or "Honey, can you bring me a tissue?" (I knew that was code for booger rocket.)

My study soon became about much more than learning to say the words in a different language. The passage was taking on a whole new meaning as it became alive with the reckless and ridiculous love of God. The lunacy of the worst deal ever made. Not because the all-knowing Maker of everything was naïvely duped, but because He was just that crazy for us.

I wrote the meaning out over and over in my own words, based on what I'd learned from the Hebrew—"Certainly, sickness He bore. He dragged suffering along as if he were greatly pregnant with it. God: beaten, slaughtered, looked down upon. He was polluted, stained, wrecked for our rebellion. For our breach of trust. He was beaten to pieces for our guilt. Punished for our favor. By his 'blueness'—the bruises, stripes, welts, wounds and scourging blows—we are completely healed."

One day a little later, while doing something menial, I noticed a flat spot on my back about half an inch long. It was light-colored and scaly. I'd had just the same sort of skin annoyance on my face years ago. The dermatologist had removed it, warning that it was precancerous.

This new spot wasn't a real concern, and I was irritated that I'd have to expend the time and effort to see the dermatologist in town, who seemed even more popular than a mall Santa. With all the busyness of our hectic routine, I completely forgot about it. Months later, I rediscovered the spot. It had grown bigger.

Oh, bother! I grimaced to myself and added a doctor visit to my already inexhaustible to-do list. And then the thought came, *I've never prayed about this.* And so I did pray, mostly out of ritual, with little or no real faith behind it.

Three days passed, and I still hadn't called to make an appointment with the dermatologist. Not in a stand of faith, mind you—I just hadn't gotten around to it. And I began playing with that little thing on my back, the way you mess with anything that crops up and begins to bug you. I walked toward the restroom, my hand running along my spine, trying to feel the spot I'd just been fiddling with a moment ago. Only I couldn't find it. I grabbed a mirror for a visual.

It was gone! There was only new pink skin where it had been. And a few hours later, *that* had turned to the sad-normal, shocking whitish color that matched the rest of my Nordic skin.

It was a reminder that God is really there, hearing even the simplest thought-prayer. But after such a high, many discouraging days followed, and all my earlier trust and resolve disappeared like a bowl of gravy that the dog lapped up. Even though I recognized that God was moving in our lives, sometimes I was so sick of our situation that I could barely keep my cool.

On one such day, I was reading *Adventures in God*, a biography about John G. Lake, a missionary to Africa who had an uncompromising faith and witnessed countless miracles (Harrison House,

1991). In later years, he opened a Healing Room in Spokane, Washington, where he prayed for the sick with such success that Spokane was soon called the healthiest city in America.

I was disheartened when I read that he had excused himself from praying for a child with a broken neck, explaining that he didn't have faith for that and he didn't want to hamper the prayers of those who did. In the end, though, the child was healed.

I groaned to God in frustration, "God, if *that* guy couldn't find faith for a broken neck, how in the world am I supposed to? He saw tons of awesome healing miracles. I haven't really seen very much stuff like that. For all this time since our accident, I've come to You morning, noon and night, pleading with You for healing and restoration for my family. And instead, it seems as if all I've got is this tiny seed of faith to cling to."

As soon as the prayer was out of my mouth, my posture changed as I began to realize fully the significance of what I had said, of what I had been given. Verses sprang to mind: "The kingdom of heaven is like a mustard seed, which a man took and planted in his field. Though it is the smallest of all your seeds, yet when it grows, it is the largest of garden plants and becomes a tree, so that the birds of the air come and perch in its branches" (Matthew 13:31–32).

"I tell you the truth, if you have faith as small as a mustard seed, you can say to this mountain, 'Move from here to there,' and it will move. Nothing will be impossible for you" (Matthew 17:20).

"He who goes out weeping, carrying seed to sow, will return with songs of joy, carrying sheaves with him" (Psalm 126:6).

"Still other seed fell on good soil, where it produced a crop—a hundred, sixty or thirty times what was sown" (Matthew 13:8).

It occurred to me that when Jesus was revealing the secrets of how things worked, He had a lot to say about seeds growing into something important. Even dark, evil things operate under that principle; sin begins as a tiny seed of thought.

That small seed of faith Jesus referred to may not have moved the mountain in its original state. But even if we can't see anything happening with our small seeds of faith, Jesus urged us throughout His teachings to believe that we've received what we pray for. He urged us not to doubt or give up! Remember, He said the tiny seed grew into a huge tree. Maybe that eensy faith seed was meant to grow when nurtured in good soil? And then it would become a major contender, bowling over all obstacles in its path!

I wanted that kind of faith! I prayed, "God, protect this microscopic seed of faith You planted in me. Cup Your own strong hands around it until it grows big enough to bravely face the elements."

The prayer brought to mind a visual—my watchful neighbor's high-yield tomato plants, carefully guarded and fussed over until harvest. I wouldn't want to be the swashbuckling teenager who dared to mess with those prized Big Boys . . .

16

RHINO REVELATIONS

Even though the afternoons were still mostly scorching hot, the mornings and evenings were cool. Autumn was here, my favorite time of year. I loved living in the Midwest with its changing of the seasons. One especially lovely fall afternoon, I was sanding a wooden chair on the deck. I'd been buying them up at flea markets for a dollar or two. I reveled in taking a dirty, gross thing and awesoming it up. It was therapeutic.

I was startled when Allen pointed out two young speckled deer unusually nearby. I cautiously stepped closer, took a knee and held my hand out to them. They began walking toward me, closer and closer, stopping ten or fifteen feet in front of me. They were so close I could see their nostrils flaring as they sniffed. They weren't frightened off when I went inside for a camera. I clicked a dozen shots. Then I moved wrong, and their white tails danced as they bounced away into a meager patch of woods. I wished Lily had been alongside me.

She was in school now, a small Christian academy. I would get so lonely for her by the end of the day that sometimes when I went to pick her up and they weren't quite done yet, it took every ounce of restraint not to burst down the door of her classroom and grab her as though she'd been held hostage at gunpoint in there.

It was coming up on her golden birthday, the one where you turn the same age as the date of your birth. She was turning six, and I couldn't believe it. She looked huge lying in bed at night, like something out of a mad scientist's lab, all legs and feet and long, thin arms. I got weepy whenever I'd spot a toddler in her momma's arms. That's how I still saw Lily, until I'd really *see* her and come back to Planet Reality.

Early on a Sunday morning, just two days before her big day, she was the first one up and I heard her happily playing in the living room. All of a sudden there was a bone-chilling scream, the one every parent knows instinctively that terrifies you. Your body lunges into rescue mode without even knowing what's wrong. I flew out of bed and down the hall, where Lily held her head in a strange way. She had a look of terror in her eyes.

She complained of dizziness, that the room was spinning, and from time to time her eyes would dart side to side involuntarily, superfast, which would cause her to panic. Right away, I put my hands on her and prayed. She threw up about four times and then fell asleep on the bathroom floor. I carried her to her bed and briefed Allen, who was still stuck in bed, left wondering what was going on. I got him up and ready as quickly as I could. He was so hurt by the fact that he couldn't help Lily, or hold and comfort her. She slept most of the afternoon.

By evening she was better, but still had headaches and dizziness. Occasionally her eyes would blitz back and forth. The optimist in me was trying to convince myself that she had a touch of the stomach virus. She had vomited that morning, after all. It was the first time I'd ever wished for anything to do with the stomach flu. But there was a sickening suspicion in the pit of me that something far worse was wrong. Allen's dad had passed away of a brain tumor.

I know exactly what you're thinking: *Why didn't you take that baby to a doctor!* Perhaps I should have. And soon I would have. But I had it on my heart to pray first. I so preferred God's healing, and I sorely dreaded putting Lily through all the worry and fear of a battery of medical tests. In deep conviction, I waited a day longer than I usually would have.

She did some better Monday afternoon—lethargic and dizzy, but better. By Monday night, however, I was worried sick. Lily still had no appetite and no energy, and she was still complaining of dizziness and a headache. Plus, the eye episodes were really scaring us. That night, Allen was meeting upstairs with two different groups of college students for Bible study. I took Lily down in the basement for a warm bath. She was so exhausted that she laid her head on the side of the tub. I had brought down some of her favorite snacks, but she still had no appetite.

After her bath, she lay down on a bed in the guest room and cried when her eyes did that crazy thing again. I snuggled close beside her to comfort her. I softly stroked her eyebrow with the side of my thumb over and over, holding her cheek in my hand, just the way my mom did when I was small. And I prayed so completely earnestly that God would heal her and spare us all this grief and worry.

She fell asleep. We were lying so close that our skin touched at the ankles and wrists, growing warm and damp. I didn't move at all until I heard every last student leave, then I carried Lily up the stairs, put her in my own bed and blubbered all my worries and concerns to Allen.

While she slept, I put my hands on her still little body and prayed what I have prayed most nights ever since she was tiny: "Father, I ask for Your blessing on Lily. Thank You for sharing her with us. Please, may Your angels guard her from all the tricks of the devil. May the blood of Jesus protect her from every sickness and disease. May she have a heart that is soft and open to Jesus. May goodness and mercy follow her all of her days. Please write her name in Your *Book of Life* . . ."

I prayed on and off through most of the night. At one point I felt an assurance from God: *The devil doesn't have permission to mess with her. He's messing with you. Trust Me.* But to be completely honest, even after that I was a weepy, worrying, slobbering mess. Even after all we'd been through, I knew losing Lily or even watching her face a terrible illness would be much, much worse than anything we had faced so far. If God would only heal her, I would be so completely happy and grateful—I couldn't imagine ever complaining about anything *ever* again.

Isn't it crazy how we always make these bargains with God when we desperately want something, deals we know we can never make good on?

I barely slept. I kept waking up and staring at her, as I did when she was a baby, half-expecting to miss some important milestone if I closed my eyes for more than five minutes. Finally, exhaustion won and I trailed off.

Lily woke me up about 5:00 A.M. It was the morning of her sixth birthday. She wanted some toast and chocolate milk, the first food she had requested since that terrible Sunday morning. I've never been so happy to crawl out of bed at dawn. It was like someone had thrown the light on in her—she was completely well—healed! I knew it immediately, even though, truth be told, I watched her like a hawk for the next several days. I felt unspeakable gratitude, tinged with lingering traces of fear, like the fork that comes through the dishwasher mostly clean except for hardened-up bits of gunk still on it. At least that's how the forks come out of my dishwasher. (Dinner, anyone?)

Lily went to school and took in snacks for everyone to celebrate her birthday. After school, she opened the gifts we'd gotten her, and then we went roller-skating with two of her little friends! She went strong all day, from 5:00 in the morning until after 9:00 that night. No more weird eye stuff, headaches or dizziness. Praise God!

At bedtime, when everyone was asleep, the Lord seemed especially real and near. I'd been reading Revelation 3:20 about how Jesus stands at the door and knocks, wanting to come in and be close to us. I'd always taken that to be an evangelistic sort of verse—something a preacher mentions during an arduous altar call, trying to persuade the fellow uncomfortably on the edge of his seat to come down the aisle. I was surprised to see that in its context, the verse was written to church folks. It reminded me of the picture in Song of Solomon, a bridegroom knocking at his bride's door.

I got down on knees to pray in the hallway, right between the linen closet and the laundry-room door, close enough to hear Allen if he needed something. Close enough to hear Lily if she needed something. It wasn't a pretty picture. First off, I was ready for bed and wore bulky glasses and monkey dorm pants. Secondly, I'd been reading in 1 Corinthians 11:4–6 about women covering their head when they pray. It was something I had never done before, but I wondered if I ought to be observing it? It's humiliating to mention, but wanting to be obedient, I grabbed a pillowcase from the linen closet and threw it on my head. I'm not really sure why I thought praying with a pillowcase on my head would somehow please God . . . I'm pretty sure He didn't think I was holier, just weirder.

I poured out my heart to Jesus: "Lord, I hope You know, I hope it goes without saying, that I want You in my heart. It belongs to You alone. I've never actually formally said, 'Hey, Jesus, You have a long-standing invite into my heart,' or whatever, but it's true, You do! You know I want You, right? Even if there was nothing else to gain in this life, not one thing except knowing You, that would be enough. That would be a treasure beyond my wildest dreams."

As I prayed, the laundry-room door opened all at once, for no apparent reason. I know there are at least a dozen rational explanations, but it startled me so badly that I leapt to my feet with that goofy pillowcase and the awful glasses on my head, hoping maybe it wasn't Jesus after all—at least not before I could get an extreme makeover.

When I got brave, I peeked behind the half-open door. Nothing electrifying. Just a mound of laundry, some lint balls and every pair of shoes we own. I was amused, and my heartfelt prayer kind of screeched to an abrupt halt as I slouched into bed, grinning inside about how goofy I must have looked wearing a pillowcase.

After such a late night, the next morning came like an unwelcome phone solicitation during Thanksgiving dinner. It was a school morning, so we really had to scoot. Lily was adjusting to school and making friends fast. If you asked her outright, she would deny that she liked it—I think in an effort to please me since I felt miserable with her gone all day.

One classmate gave her a jar, the kind we were all familiar with as kids. It had holes punched in the top and bits of grass, leaves and twigs inside. Lily pointed out a caterpillar and a chrysalis in the jar. I took her word for it. I could see the fuzzy worm just fine, but I was pretty sure the other thing she pointed to was just a dirt clod. I'd seen a marvelous chrysalis online once—the "Golden Chrysalis" in Australia, almost metallic-looking and brilliant. But this thing looked dead-dead. Brown. Dirtish. It just rolled around on the floor of the bug keeper she'd transferred everything to.

She took votes, trying to nail down a name for the caterpillar, who seemed much more exciting and alive than the dirt clod. "Rhino?" she inquired. "Or Spike?" After a few days, she lost interest in the little guy. I put him up on top of the refrigerator to rescue him from the curious cat, who kept trying to knock him off the desk for a better look at whether or not he was edible.

Even though it shouldn't have been a big shock, I was flabbergasted when I spotted a little butterfly in the container some days after that, on one of my many trips to study the contents of the refrigerator. I screamed and squealed and called everyone to come see. On closer inspection, we noticed that Rhino had changed into a chrysalis that same day, just as ugly and dead-looking as the other one had been, as if he realized that maybe it wasn't that bad a process after all.

We all gathered on the front porch to bid farewell to the little butterfly. With great pomp, Lily opened the door of the bug keeper. He fluttered out crooked and cockeyed and sat on a wicker chair for a long while to let his wings dry. After twenty minutes, dry and ready, he flew a circle around the whole yard, turned back and—I kid you not—landed on Lily's collarbone, tickling her cheek with his wings as if to say good-bye. Then he flew off for good. We watched him as long as we could, all misty-eyed over the little fella whose life had seemed as good as gone. He danced from flower to flower in complete, buggy delight.

I was pleased to see that Lily had inherited the cheese factor from me. She said something thoughtful and idealistic along the lines of, "That's just like people. They turn into something way better after they die!" And I contemplated how new life *always* gets its start in dark places—a cocoon, an egg, a womb, the dirt and yes, even tragedy

I thought about that for a long time as I reflected on this weird journey we'd been on. I could never begin to explain why God works the way He does. Sometimes, it's a lot of "fast and flash" with loads of pizzazz. Other times, it's silently, with long spells of not much happening and no progress to report. A lot like the Weather Channel, actually.

God is quirky that way. Mysterious all right, but always good. And later, as I tried to imagine how our story would end, I hung on with tenacity to that picture of the butterfly flying far-off into the neighbor's yard and beyond. As good as our life had been so far, I knew it was nothing like the one God has planned for our future. Even though we were now in a waiting stage in our lives, I fully believed that in God's time and in His way, He would make something lovely of us yet.

The End. Sort of.

ABOUT THE AUTHOR

Christina Schofield describes herself this way: I am mostly nervous. Smallish. Nearsighted. Often shy. I doodle. My voice is soft, and I am plain-looking. I hate talking on the phone. I love pickles and noodles and chocolate (not all at once). I am loyal. Forgiving. Disorganized. Quirky. Forgetful. Sometimes I sing into hairbrush microphones. I went to Africa once, but I've never been to Vegas. I like small towns—Rolla, Missouri, fits me just fine.

Did I mention I'm forgetful? I like thrift stores and garage sales. I wear a T-shirt and jeans almost every day, and the same pair of sneakers. I am terrible at the laundry and an awful cook. I am infatuated with my family. My daughter, Lily, and I are arguably the worst two dancers ever. I have a soft spot for robots, sharpened pencils and the smell of fall. I am a terrible driver. And I am completely in love with God.

Sometimes God lets me draw pictures for kids' books and write things. People even pay me sometimes. The people at Standard Publishing, Group Publishing and Zonderkidz are some of them. (Thanks, guys.) My favorite stuff to do: hanging out with family and making music to God. Things I avoid: technology, snow skiing and, ironically, talking about myself.

277.3SC   1109111 $12.99

Scriver